—— Along the Arun ——

John Adamson

The Alexius Press

A CIP catalogue record for this book is available from the British Library

© *John Adamson 1994*

ISBN: 0 9519886 1 1

Typeset by Susan Woolliams Desktop Publishing Services, Woodbridge, Suffolk.

Printed and bound by the Lowfield Printing Company Ltd., Crayford, Dartford, Kent.

Published by
THE ALEXIUS PRESS LIMITED, 1994

The Cover: *Clockwise from top left: South Terrace, Littlehampton; Arundel High Street; the Arun from Houghton Bridge; Stopham Bridge.*

Reproduced from colour slides taken by Andrew Bucknall.

CONTENTS

LIST OF ILLUSTRATIONS

Unless otherwise stated below all photographs were taken by Andrew Bucknall.

LIST OF MAPS

> *Key*
> ▬ ▬ ▬   Recommended route   **+** Church or chapel
>
> . . . .   Alternative route proposed in text

The maps were drawn by Kate Wilson.

PREFACE

For more than twenty years I have visited the Arun Valley area of West Sussex. It has seemed to me a place of inexhaustible fascination, with beauty of landscape associated with works of man rich in architectural and historical interest. An element of mystery is an important factor in the area's attraction for me; the villages half-hidden by trees, the windings and diversions of the Arun itself; glimpsed first from car or train, these things would, I felt sure, repay exploration.

As I came to know the area better, the idea of this book evolved. The structure was to be a series of walks from Littlehampton at the mouth of the Arun up to Pulborough. To do justice to the area, it seemed to me that something more than a typical walkers' guide was needed; something which filled in the complex historical background to what we now see. Arundel, in particular, appeared to require an exposition which dovetailed the history of the Earls of Arundel and Dukes of Norfolk, of the Castle which dominates the town, and of the town itself.

The book as it is now presented to the reader can certainly be used as a guide for those who like fairly long walks. However, many people - particularly those with cars - may well prefer to walk only comparatively short sections of the route, concentrating on places which are readily accessible and strike them as of particular interest. I hope also that there will be appeal to the armchair traveller with a bent for local history.

One of the pleasures of writing this book has been the friendly and supportive attitude of so many of the people I have encountered while working on it, and thanks are due to them and to friends for their encouragement. I should like in particular to acknowledge the assistance given to my research by Timothy McCann, Assistant County Archivist at the West Sussex Record Office, Joyce Crow, Honorary Librarian of the Sussex Archaeological Society, the staff of the Littlehampton Museum and the staff of the British Library and the London Library. I need hardly

1

say that the responsibility for what is written in this book remains exclusively the author's. I am also most grateful for the sterling work of Barbara Kulesza, who typed the manuscript through more drafts than I care to remember. Acknowledgement is made to The Marvell Press, publishers of the poems of Philip Larkin, for permission to use the extract from "An Arundel Tomb" which appears on page 53.

Finally, I hope that readers derive as much pleasure from exploring the Arun Valley as I have done.

John Adamson

London
May 1994

INTRODUCTION

Natural features of the landscape such as rivers and hills are not just the background to people's lives today, but form a link with the innumerable generations which have preceded us, and beyond them with periods of time whose distance is difficult for the mind to grasp, over which the Earth took its present form. It is, for example, superficially strange that the River Arun, like its Sussex neighbours the Adur, the Ouse and the Cuckmere, arises not in the high ground of the South Downs, but in the comparatively flat land of the Weald. To understand how that situation has arisen we need to go back to a time between 110 and 65 million years ago when Sussex and, at times, most of England, was under the sea. During that time chalk, which consists mainly of crystals secreted by planktonic algae, was deposited. Earth movements then lifted the chalk into the shape of a dome over what is now the Weald, with what became the North and South Downs forming a rim. The Arun and its neighbours rose on that dome, and gained there the momentum which enabled them to cut their way through the Downland valleys where they now run. The chalk which formed the centre of the dome was then eroded, leaving the rivers to pursue their placid courses with only a modest fall between their headwaters and the sea.

As this book was about to go to press, the announcement was made of the discovery at Boxgrove near Chichester of the shin bone of a human ancestor, hailed by the media as Boxgrove Man, who is thought to have lived some 500,000 years ago. Sussex can therefore claim to have provided the evidence of the first known Briton, perhaps indeed the first known European. Traces had previously been found of Palaeolithic people who lived some 100,000 years after Boxgrove Man. The next phase of human occupation of the Sussex area was that of the Mesolithic hunter-gatherers whose culture was largely replaced during the period 5000 - 3000 B.C. by that of Neolithic farmers. We have much more evidence of the people of the Bronze and Iron Ages - regarded as stretching from late in the second millenium B.C. to the Roman occupation - including the outlines of their fields, indicated by banks or "lynchets". The Belgae, an Iron Age people who arrived about 75 B.C., may well have founded a city on the coastal plain in the Selsey area. No trace remains of that, but within the area covered by this book evidence of the Belgae survives in the Arundel area, as mentioned in Chapter 6. It is the Belgae who provide us with the first recorded name of a political leader who held sway over what we now call Sussex - Commius, King of the Atrebates, a tribe whose area of control stretched along the South Coast between the present-day towns of Eastbourne and Bournemouth, and ran north as far as the Berkshire Downs. Commius had previously been King of the Atrebates in Gaul, and was sent to Britain by Julius Caesar as a preliminary to his inconclusive invasions which took place in 55 and 54 B.C. Commius returned to Gaul with Caesar in the latter year but then changed sides, joining the revolt of the Gauls under Vercingetorix, escaping back to Britain when the revolt failed.

Following the death of Commius the Kingdom of the Atrebates broke up, and when the next - and decisive - Roman invasion took place in 43 A.D., under the general Aulus Plautius who had been sent by the Emperor Claudius, there was something of a re-run of the political situation which obtained at the time of Caesar's invasion. As on that occasion the Romans, while facing some hostile tribes, could rely on a degree of British support. In the Claudian invasion, the rôle previously adopted by Commius of the Atrebates was taken by Cogidubnus of the Regni, the name given to that part of the Atrebates who were centred on what is now Sussex.

Cogidubnus had his reward in being established by the Romans as what the British in India would have called a "Native Prince". He remained loyal to Rome during the revolt of the Iceni under Boudicca, and his status and the regard in which he was held by the Romans is illustrated by the Palace at Fishbourne which was almost certainly his headquarters during the latter part of his reign. It was possibly during the reign of Cogidubnus that the Regni established their capital at the site of what is now Chichester. In Roman times that city was known as Noviomagus, a Celtic name meaning "new city on the plain", illustrating the fact that although it was typically Roman in its plan and its features such as Ampitheatre, Forum and Basilica, it was not a directly and exclusively Roman foundation. The name Chichester, which sounds of Roman origin, comes in fact from a

4

Saxon root, possibly deriving from Cissa the son of Aelle the invader of Sussex mentioned below - although it has been suggested that the writer of the Anglo-Saxon Chronicle to whom we owe Cissa's name may, in fact, have invented the person to explain the place name.

Stane Street, the Roman road from Chichester to London, crosses the route of the walk in this book, and a Roman fortified post, described in Chapter 11, is close to the route. Also on Stane Street, and near the area covered by this book, is the large Roman villa at Bignor which has fine mosaic pavements. While this villa would have been the centre of a substantial estate, like those subsequently constituting manors, much of the countryside remained in the possession of individual farmers continuing broadly the pattern of life they would have had before the Romans arrived.

The collapse of Roman authority in the early fifth century A.D. left the Romano-British inhabitants of Sussex, as of the rest of Britain, struggling to maintain their society in the face of political uncertainty and military threat. The written and archaeological evidence of subsequent events in Sussex is sketchy. The Saxons under their leader Aelle may have settled initially under treaty, or as conquerors from the beginning; the date of their arrival (thought to have been on the Selsey peninsula) is given by the *Anglo-Saxon Chronicle* as 477; although recent scholarship has suggested a date twenty years earlier than that. The subsequent Saxon conquest lacked the speed and decisiveness of the Roman which preceded it and the Norman which followed; according to the chronology of the *Anglo-Saxon Chronicle*, it took the Saxons fourteen years to reach and take the fort of Pevensey.

There has been much scholarly debate about the extent to which there was a continuity of development between Romano-British and Anglo-Saxon society. The evidence is not, and never can be, conclusive. Those who feel the strong sense of continuity with the past evident even in modern Sussex, and can appreciate the great isolation of individual families and communities which must have been a feature of a Sussex whose landscape included much forest and swamp, are likely to suspect that however great the political upheavals which historians now strive to understand, the life of many of the common people will have continued on lines which had been set for many generations.

The Saxons have left their mark in the Arun Valley in the form of the fortified site at Burpham, described in Chapter 8. A Saxon origin is also claimed for Arundel Castle although no trace of Saxon work remains. The Saxons' defences were built against Viking/Danish raiders; in due course it was such raiders who had settled in France and achieved comparative respectability as Normans who were to conquer England.

The South Saxons briefly re-established as a political unit the territory which had been occupied by the Regni, but following a battle in 607 they became tributary to the West Saxon kingdom, and never regained full independence during the often confusing shifts of power which marked the centuries before the Norman Conquest. Sussex did not, however, by any means drift into isolation from national politics. Godwin, who is thought to have been the son of the Sussex thane Wulfnoth, was Earl of Wessex and one of the most powerful men in the kingdom during the latter part of the reign of Cnut (1016 - 35), the reigns of Cnut's sons Harold (1035 - 40) and Harthacnut (1040 - 42), and the early part of that of Edward the Confessor (1042 - 66); Edward married his daughter Edith in 1045. Six years later he fell from favour; his career curiously prefiguring those of some of the Earls of Arundel and Dukes of Norfolk described later in this book, except that Godwin was sufficiently strong, and disloyal, to force the King to restore him to his position of power.

Godwin's son Harold achieved such a position as political figure and military leader that he became King after the death of Edward the Confessor. In accordance with Edward's wish and with the support of the leading figures in the country he succeeded to the throne in spite of not being in the royal line of succession. It was from Bosham, one of the Sussex manors which he had inherited from his father, and from which Godwin had gone into exile in 1051, that Harold had set sail on the expedition to Normandy during which he is claimed to have sworn loyalty to Duke William - a sequence of events recounted in the Bayeux Tapestry. Whatever the precise significance of these preliminaries to the Norman Conquest, the outcome is, of course, well known - the invasion of England by William, and his victory at Hastings, in 1066.

An important thread of continuity between the Saxons and Normans was provided by the Christian Church. In 681 - 84 years after St. Augustine of

6

Canterbury had started his mission in Kent - St. Wilfred and a band of followers had landed on the Selsey peninsula and initiated the conversion of the South Saxons. They were given land at Selsey which became the seat of the South Saxon bishopric. In 1076 the seat was moved to Chichester but the boundaries of the bishopric remained the same. In ecclesiastical architecture, it is often difficult to distinguish Saxon from early Norman work.

After the Conquest, Sussex was divided by William the Conqueror among his nobles; Arundel was the base for Roger de Montgomery's share of the county. Chapter 4, in following the history of the Earls of Arundel, gives some indication of the subsequent political events which would have impacted on the people of Sussex, although much normal life must have continued uninterrupted by the conflicts mentioned. More serious disruption was almost certainly caused by the French invasion of 1216 in support of barons in revolt against King John; it was not until the next year, after the King's death, that the invaders were driven out.

Troubles with the French recurred during the second half of the fourteenth century when raiding was frequent, and in Chapter 9 there is reference to that time in relation to the fortification of Amberley Castle. The naval exploits of Richard twelfth Earl of Arundel mentioned in Chapter 1 were in reaction - albeit rather belated - to the threat of raids and perhaps invasion.

Amid the uncertainties of medieval life stood the Church, the pervasive influence of which was evident not only in the parish churches and diocesan organisation but in monastic institutions, in which Sussex was particularly rich - some feature in this book. For a time these institutions must have seemed part of the natural order of things, set to endure for many centuries. The reality proved very different.

In the 1340s, Sussex, like the rest of England, was struck by the plague known as the Black Death. Its effects - compounded by those of the French raids mentioned above - were devastating in many aspects of the county's life, social, economic and religious. Up to a half of the county's population is thought to have died as a result of the Black Death's most virulent impact, in 1348 - 49; monastic institutions were struck like other sectors of the population. Many villages were deserted; although curiously enough, none in the Arun Valley, unlike that of the Adur, only some thirteen miles away.

The combined effects of plague, war, poverty and oppression led to the peasants' revolt of 1381. There was an impact in Sussex even though it was not one of those counties mainly affected. Although in the next century Sussex was again involved in an irruption of popular anger - Jack Cade's rebellion of 1450, which was motivated by a mixture of political and economic grievances - in general the fifteenth century in Sussex saw economic improvement and the consolidation of civil society, helped by the county's comparative immunity from the upheavals of the Wars of the Roses; and in secular society progress was maintained in the sixteenth century.

The story was very different in the religious sphere. The idealism of the monastic movement had waned with the passage of time, and within that movement - as indeed within the Church as a whole - a spirit of service had tended to be replaced by remoteness, laxity of observance, and pursuit of wealth. When, during the reign of Henry VIII, Cardinal Wolsey and then Thomas Cromwell set out to close monastic institutions and appropriate their property, therefore, they were able in many parts of England, including Sussex, to do so without, in general, a great deal of public protest.

Later in this book references are to be found to a number of monastic institutions which fell victim at the time of the Reformation. While views on the usefulness of the monastic way of life vary, many people will feel in contemplating the ruins of monastic houses some sense of loss at a tradition destroyed; also, in an age which has seen many upheavals of its own, some sympathy with the monks, friars and nuns rudely uprooted from their (usually) cloistered existence. Happily, many were redeployed, as we should say nowadays, into parish work; others received pensions.

Continued religious tensions are reflected in the story of the Dukes of Norfolk as set out in Chapter 4, and in divisions within Sussex society which affected the attitude people took at the time of the Civil War. In that

8

conflict Sussex was not the site of any major battles, but there were a number of clashes of arms in the area - those at Arundel being described in Chapter 6. Although there was some settling of Civil War scores after the restoration of Charles II, in general a comparatively gentlemanly attitude was adopted throughout a turbulent period during which districts, classes and families were divided in their loyalties.

The eighteenth century was something of a golden age for aristocratic Sussex families, whose wealth and taste were demonstrated in building and landscaping, and whose influence was exercised through artistic patronage and political activity. In the latter part of the century, the fashion for sea bathing led to the development of seaside resorts - Chapter 1 refers to this process in relation to Littlehampton.

Beneath this calm surface, however, there was much turbulence. Agricultural depression and enclosure led to impoverishment, and a major source of employment in the county was smuggling. While this activity has acquired a certain romantic aura, the reality was much grimmer, with smugglers employing intimidation backed by murder to enforce acquiescence in their activities, and a number of pitched battles being fought between smugglers and the forces of law and order.

In the early nineteenth century, pressure caused by overpopulation and poverty, and exacerbated by the effects of a system which placed responsibility for relief of the poor on the individual parish, led to discontent which culminated in the "Captain Swing" rioting of 1830. The Poor Law Amendment Act of 1834, by grouping parishes for the relief of poverty, and greater economic activity related particularly to development in transport, led to improved conditions, and Sussex settled into a less turbulent era.

Up to the early eighteenth century Sussex had been notorious for the poor condition of its roads, crossing the Weald being very hazardous in winter. Later in that century there was a great improvement in Sussex roads because of the building of turnpikes, run by Turnpike Trusts which were authorised to levy tolls on road users. Nevertheless, in an era when road travel was by horse-drawn coach, the benefits of road improvements for the personal traveller (there were also benefits for the farmers) were very much concentrated on the well-off; in no way did a system of mass

9

transport exist, and facilities for movement of large amounts of freight remained very inadequate.

The nineteenth century saw a remarkable improvement in what we should now call the transport infrastructure. Earlier measures to facilitate the navigation of rivers were supplemented - the action taken in respect of the lower Arun is described in this book. Canals were built, in Sussex notably the Wey and Arun, which naturally increased trade on both rivers, but also one linking the Arun with Portsmouth, to which reference is made in Chapter 3. Far more significant, of course, was the creation of the railway network, which had a profound effect in terms of economic development, and also in terms of the impact on individuals and local communities in providing greatly increased personal mobility. The chalk pits at Amberley, described in Chapter 9, are an example of an industry which benefited successively from canal and railway development.

Inevitably, improved communications, notably in terms of transport but also of large circulation newspapers, radio and in due course television, had the effects of reducing the isolation and distinctiveness of Sussex, as of other parts of England. To attempt to describe the social and political development of Sussex over the last, say, 150 years would, to a large extent, be to record the local impact of national trends and events. Nevertheless, Sussex has retained much of its own character, particularly in areas such as the Arun Valley, which have not been heavily affected by that spread of often ill-planned urban developments which has been one of the less happy features of the county in the twentieth century. To maintain this character without stopping necessary change and development is a major challenge. In meeting it a balanced understanding of the past must be an asset.

In the chapters which follow, the threads of the early history of the Arun valley area will be linked with more recent events and with the contemporary scene in a personal interpretation of this beautiful and historically rich part of England. No such interpretation can ever hope to be definitive; both the current scene and perspective on the past are subject to constant change. It is hoped, however, that this account will be found both informative and enjoyable.

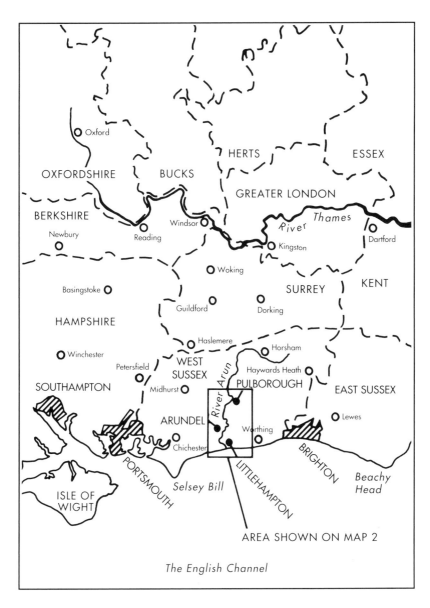

AREA SHOWN ON MAP 2

The English Channel

Southern England, showing location of the Arun valley.
Scale 1: 1,188,000 - 18.75 miles to one inch.

CHAPTER 1. History of Littlehampton

Littlehampton has the holiday attractions of modern Sussex: beach, amusement park, yachts on the river, open country for walkers. Unlike some other South Coast resorts, however, Littlehampton is not simply the product of the relatively recent desire of the English to take their holidays by the sea. It was originally a port, and existed as such in Saxon times under the name Hamtun; the "Little" was a medieval addition, possibly to distinguish the town from Southampton. After the Norman Conquest it was active in the import of stone from quarries in Caen and as the English landfall of great figures of the day. William Rufus landed in Littlehampton in 1097 after campaigning in France and Matilda, daughter of Henry I, is thought to have arrived here in 1139 on her way to Arundel during her campaign to assert her right to the English throne against Stephen. It was also prominent later in the Middle Ages. Richard Fitzalan, the eleventh Earl of Arundel and a major military and naval figure, brought to Littlehampton prisoners taken at the Battle of Crécy in 1346. In 1387 his son, also Richard, who as mentioned in Chapter 4 was Admiral of England, defeated a fleet of Flemings, Frenchmen and Spaniards off Margate, capturing many ships, and went on to capture more on a raiding expedition to Sluis; some of these ships were brought to Littlehampton.

At that time the Arun was not set in its present course, and its mouth was some way to the east of its present position. It has been argued indeed that it was at one time as far to the east as Worthing, but the evidence for this falls short of the conclusive. We can, however, envisage medieval Littlehampton as being not directly on the sea but on a tidal estuary which was separated from the sea by a shingle bank. So far as can be understood, the tendency of the river mouth to be pushed east by the drift of the shingle in that direction was counteracted by the river's propensity to break through the shingle bank to the sea when erosion permitted.

The river appears to have found access to the sea at Littlehampton in the early sixteenth century, no doubt as part of that phase of erosion which led

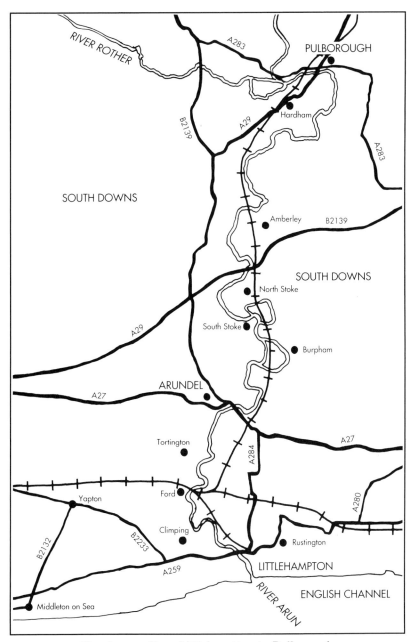

The Arun valley - Littlehampton to Pulborough.
Scale 1:158,400 - 2.5 miles to one inch.

to the disappearance of the village of Cudlow, as mentioned in Chapter 3. This outlet was consolidated when in the 1570s Henry Fitzalan, twentieth Earl of Arundel, embanked the lower Arun.

The problems posed by shifting sands around the mouth of the Arun were however intractable. By the end of the seventeenth century the river was again following a circuitous route as it reached the sea, and in 1732 an Act of Parliament provided for a new channel to be cut to the sea with piers on either side to protect it. Further Acts of Parliament proved necessary to maintain the harbour and regulate the way in which it was run.

The steps taken were effective in maintaining Littlehampton's position as a port. In the nineteenth century formidable families of ship builders, repairers and owners, the Isemongers, Harveys and Robinsons, dominated the commercial life of the town; the paintings and other exhibits in the Littlehampton Museum convey the flavour of that era. As the glories of the age of sail faded in the face of competition from steam, however, Littlehampton's family shipping firms faded also, although the G. and J. Robinson company continued into the 1920s.

The middle of the nineteenth century saw a marked increase in activity in Littlehampton harbour as a result of the opening in 1863 of the town's railway station and, as a consequence of that, of the establishment of ferry services to the Continent. These services only lasted some twenty years, however, as they were unable to survive competition from those based at other south coast ports, especially Newhaven. While the harbour continued in substantial use particularly for the handling of agricultural products, timber, and coal, a decline set in, which was only briefly arrested during the First World War when it was used for loading war materials required in France.

The town - originally village - centre of Littlehampton was at some distance from both the sea and the river. The course previously taken by the Arun, as already indicated, explains why the village was not built by the sea. The tendency of the Arun to flood was no doubt a main factor in determining that the village should be some way to the east of the line of the river. In medieval times - and indeed as late as the second half of the seventeenth century - the village appears to have consisted only of a church, manor house and small number of houses grouped round a triangular area which probably served as market place and village green. As indicated in the following chapter, the plan of this original core of the town may still be seen in contemporary Littlehampton.

By the beginning of the eighteenth century the town was expanding to the west, but remaining to the north of the line of what is now the New Road until the Arun's new channel was cut following the 1732 Act. We can envisage the working life of Littlehampton at that time as based partly on agriculture and partly on the harbour.

The second half of the eighteenth century saw the development of a new rôle for Littlehampton which has continued until the present time - that of seaside resort. The attractions of sea bathing were identified in 1750 in Richard Russell's *A Dissertation concerning the use of Sea-Water in the Diseases of the Glands*, and visiting the seaside became fashionable first at Brighton and then at other towns. In the eighteenth century as now, refreshments and accommodation were needed for visitors. A pioneer in providing these at Littlehampton was Peter Le Cocq, a London coffee-house owner, who ran the Beach Hotel.

As with other seaside resorts, the end of the eighteenth century and the early part of the nineteenth saw a flurry of building to cater for those who wished to own or rent fashionable properties. This process started in the 1790s at the north-east of the Green, at Norfolk Place, and extended west along South Terrace, although progress became stately in pace - St. Augustine's Road was not reached until the 1870s. The phasing of the Terrace can be detected in the changing architectural style. Beach Town, as this area was called, was separated from the rest of Littlehampton not only by open space but also by some social distance.

The opening of Littlehampton Station in 1863, already mentioned in connection with the development of the harbour, and the improvement of the railway service following the establishment of the loop line at Ford in 1887, which ended the need for shunting between Littlehampton and the main line, were major factors in the expansion of the tourist trade and of the town itself in the latter part of the nineteenth century. The harbour, the old town centre, and Beach Town merged into a single built-up area.

This aerial view of part of Littlehampton shows the Arun winding inland fr
on the opposite (west) side of

estuary: the pier (slightly left of centre in the picture), and the busy yacht basin
er, shown in close up on page 25.

The twentieth century has seen continued development of tourism - a significant step being the opening of the Butlin Amusement Park in 1933 - not to everyone's liking but locating Littlehampton firmly in the realm of popular taste. Modern Littlehampton is not however simply a tourist resort. To the north is a flourishing industrial area. The harbour continues its commercial life. Boats are repaired; gravel which has been sucked up from the sea bed is unloaded; and fishing activity is maintained. One may hope that in the changes which are bound to come to Littlehampton there will continue to be a healthy balance between different aspects of the town, and that the best of the old will be preserved without stifling modern commercial development essential to the economic health of the area.

South Terrace, Littlehampton.

CHAPTER 2. Walk around Littlehampton

Distance:	*About a mile and a half.*
Walking Conditions:	*Mostly roads; some firm paths.*
Station:	*Littlehampton.*

Littlehampton Station is a convenient starting point for an exploration of the town. From the forecourt, the route crosses the main road (Terminus Road) and runs down Terminus Place to River Road and then turns to the left. On the right are commercial premises lining the Arun, many awaiting redevelopment. A short distance along on the left is No. 12A, which formerly housed the Littlehampton Museum (now in the Manor House). It was built about 1904 by Captain Arthur Robinson, one of the Robinson family mentioned in Chapter 1, next door to his father Joseph's house.

River Road runs into Surrey Street. To the right, on the other side of that Street, are two buildings attached to each other but standing in splendid isolation. The one in red brick is the late eighteenth century Old Quay House; next to it is the early nineteenth century Cairo Club in blue bricks. At the end of the Cairo Club, looking left, the mouth of the Arun can be seen. The route returns along Surrey Street. To the east, as Surrey Street approaches the New Road, is Floyd's Corner. The name derives from Floyd's cycle and engineering stores, which used to occupy part of the terrace of buildings, now being redeveloped, on the right of Surrey Street.

The route continues to the right along Pier Road, built on the river embankment. To the left is the timber and building yard of Travis and Perkins. The road was originally known as Mussel Row. On the river frontage, trips up the Arun and round the harbour are on offer. At the end of Pier Road there is a pond recently used for sailing model boats and for canoes, known as the oyster pond because its original purpose was to store oysters. Beyond the pond there used to stand a windmill which was

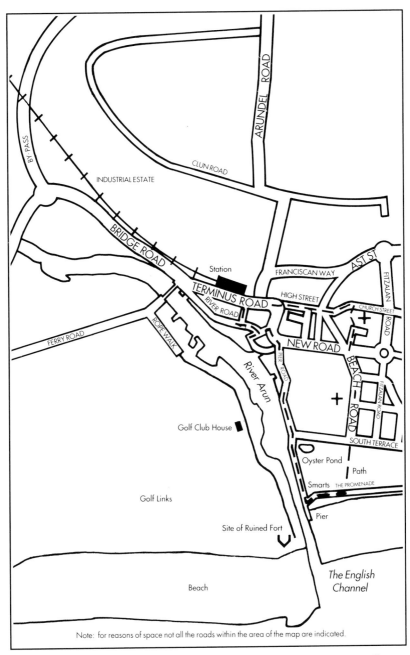

Town map of Littlehampton.   Scale 1:15,600 - 4 inches to one mile.

a feature of the Littlehampton scene from 1831 to 1932 when it was demolished by Butlins to make way for their Amusement Park which remains today, run by Smarts. The route continues along the embankment. At the south west corner of the Park may be seen the site - now faced by an embankment covered with shrubs - of a fort built in 1759 during the Seven Years' War, at a time when a French invasion seemed imminent. The threat of such invasion was only finally dispelled by Hawke's decisive victory over the French fleet at Quiberon Bay in November of that year. This fort saw further service as part of England's defences during the Napoleonic wars, but fell into obsolescence and decay during the course of the nineteenth century. A particular difficulty was restriction of the field of fire by buildings to the rear of the battery. The fort was replaced by the one on the west bank of the Arun which is mentioned in the following chapter.

The route follows the bank of the river past the lighthouse to the end of the short pier, from where there are fine views, including one of the line of the South Downs. It then returns past the coastguard station and left across the Green, by way of a tarmac path. From the Green there are views of South Terrace, mentioned in Chapter 1, and the walk can, of course, be extended in that direction. At the end of the path, the route crosses the main road to Beach Road.

Beach Road passes the modest but pleasing Marine Gardens and then St. Catherine's Roman Catholic Church, a grey stone building with a slate roof, past which is Coffyn's Field, an open, mainly grassed area. Just beyond that, at a road junction, is the well-maintained War Memorial.

Across the junction to the right is the Civic Centre, headquarters of the Arun District Council. The route follows Church Approach by the side of the Civic Centre to St. Mary's Church. It is possible that there was a Saxon Church on this site, but the first Church here of which we have firm knowledge was a medieval building with a squat tower rising from about half-way up the roof. A complete rebuilding took place in 1826 and the Church was again rebuilt in 1934. The fourteenth century east window survived the successive transformations of the Church and having at one point formed part of a garden rockery it is now placed on the west side of the tower underneath the clock, and is looking somewhat eroded. The path through the churchyard is followed into Church Street, where the route continues to the left. On the right is the Friends Meeting House, originally an infants school built at her own expense by a Mrs Welch, who purchased the site in 1835. Her school was known as a "Penny-a-week" one, after the amount which pupils were expected to contribute to cover the costs.

The Friends Meeting House in Church Street, Littlehampton.

On the left is the Manor House built in the 1830s on the site of that mentioned in Chapter 1, and containing local offices and the Littlehampton Museum, which has interesting paintings, maps and artefacts illustrative of various aspects of Littlehampton's past. At the junction opposite, the route follows to the right along Church Street where there is a pleasing line of cottages. Nos. 7 and 9 - formerly a single farmhouse - are the earliest of these buildings, dating from 1700. Vine Cottage - No. 1 - can be dated from its plaque which shows it to have been built in 1727. Nos. 11 and 13 - Fuchsia Cottage and Regency Cottage - probably date from the late eighteenth or early nineteenth century. The Gratwicke Arms takes its name from a family of Sussex landowners, one member of which is mentioned in the next chapter as the builder of Tortington House.

At the end of Church Street the route turns left into East Street. The junction between that road, originally North Street, and the High Street, originally West Street, used to be known as Smart's Corner, after a Neville Smart who started a business there in 1836, providing a multiplicity of goods and services. A subsequent owner remodelled the building but retained the original bay window, which remains today. To the right a little beyond Smart's Corner, 65 High Street, which has a squared flint facade and now incorporates a wine store, was home to the Constable brewing family who acquired it in the 1850s. They had a brewery behind the house - it was not demolished until 1972. On the other side of the road, No. 72 is a pleasing mid-nineteenth century building, now serving as a shop supplying gardeners and animal owners.

As one continues west along the High Street the road loses some of the character it has at the east end, but it retains greater interest than many such modern shopping streets.

At the end of the pedestrian section of the High Street, the route continues straight on along Terminus Road to the station. The Arun footbridge, the beginning of the route set out in the next chapter, is found by taking a left turn from Terminus Road a short way past the station between the Steam Packet and the Arun View Inn. The bridge is at the site of two earlier solutions to the problem of crossing the river. The first of these was the chain ferry, installed in 1825. This was, in effect, a piece of roadway laid on top of a boat which was pulled across the river by a chain controlled by hand-operated machinery. It was subject to some modernisation around 1870, and was replaced by a swing bridge built alongside, which was opened in 1908. This had a fixed span on the west side and, on the town side, a movable one to permit the passage of shipping. In due course fewer and fewer ships went up to Arundel, and when in 1938 the Ford railway bridge (which previously had a moveable span) was fixed, ships could no longer go beyond there. The swing bridge was replaced by the present footbridge in 1981, road traffic now being catered for by a new bridge to the north.

The busy yacht basin at Littlehampton.

CHAPTER 3. Littlehampton to Arundel

Distance: *About seven and three-quarter miles.*
Walking Conditions: *Quite firm paths; beach; roads, some busy.*
Stations: *Littlehampton, Ford, Arundel.*

Across the Arun footbridge, from which the unloading of gravel on the east bank of the river can sometimes be watched, the route turns left into Rope Walk, where, as the name suggests, rope was once made. The process used was the laborious one of twisting hemp by hand. At the end of Rope Walk, a path to the left marked "Public Footpath to West Bank $^1/_2$", brings one back to the bank of the river. After passing stretches of water/mudflats with several sunken boats one comes to the Arun Yacht Club. The yachts make a fine sight, with the masts forming interesting patterns. Opposite the pier and on the edge of the golf course is what remains of Littlehampton Fort, built in 1854 as a defence against a possible French invasion. It is a curiosity that in that very year Britain and France were fighting as allies in the Crimea. The planning of the fort derived, however, from long recognition of the obsolescence of the fort on the east bank of the Arun, mentioned in the previous chapter, and had been accelerated by concern about the ambitions of Louis Napoleon in the period after he came to power in December 1851 - although if he had emulated his uncle's plans to invade this country that would have been somewhat ungrateful, as he had escaped to England from imprisonment in France in 1846. This west bank fort itself came, however, to seem inadequate, and with the diminution of the French threat it became something of a "white elephant". The guns were removed, and much of the fort dismantled, in 1891.

Beyond the golf course are the sand dunes and a mainly shingle beach known together as West Beach. There are not many stretches of such undeveloped coast left in West Sussex. In the light of this, and because

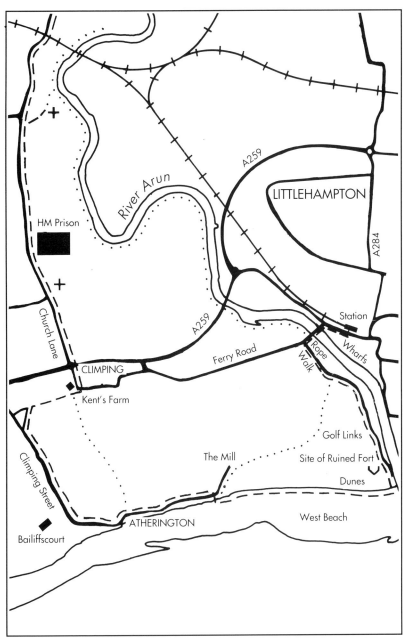

Route map, section 1: Littlehampton to Arundel, part A.
Scale 1:25,000 - 2.5 inches to one mile.

27

of the variety of plants adapted to living on the dunes, and of the way in which the soft muds and sands on the foreshore provide food for wintering birds, West Beach is a Site of Special Scientific Interest. There is a path through the dunes, but the recommended route runs directly down to the shore and then along it. Walking to the west, one can muse on the fate of the lost village of Cudlow, which disappeared at the end of the sixteenth century after a long period of erosion by the sea; its site is now probably some half mile beyond the shore line. Not much is known of its Church, which was probably late Norman and of Caen stone. We do, however, have a record of the Rectors, no less than three of whom (at the end of the fourteenth and beginning of the fifteenth century) were excommunicated for non-payment of Church taxes. No doubt it was the poverty of the village which led to this unusual situation.

A trace of Cudlow remains in John Norden's 1606 estate map of Athering-ton Manor. The land between the Arun and what is now a footpath leading north-east from the beach past the former Climping Mill back to Rope Walk was known as "East Cudlow"; a stretch of land beyond Atherington was known as "West Cudlow". The incursion of the sea had divided these two elements of what had once been a single parish.

The route continues for about one and a quarter miles along the beach, passing several sections of concrete defences. After about three-quarters of a mile a road runs behind the beach, and this provides more comfort-able walking than the pebbles. One reaches in due course car parks close to the beach, behind which are some flint barns, currently under restora-tion, which, with a few houses, constitute today's Atherington. The route follows the road through Atherington. On the left, after a short distance, is the remarkable phenomenon of Bailiffscourt.

Bailiffscourt owes its origin, and its name, to a monastic foundation by the Abbey of Séez, in Normandy; the monk who lived at the grange at this site was known as the bailiff of Atherington. Only the chapel, a late thirteenth century building, dates from that time. The manor house in fifteenth century style was built in 1935, along with two adjacent buildings in early medieval style. The other buildings in the grounds, apart from the chapel, and the pigeon house, which is probably eighteenth century, have been imported to form a sort of open-air museum.

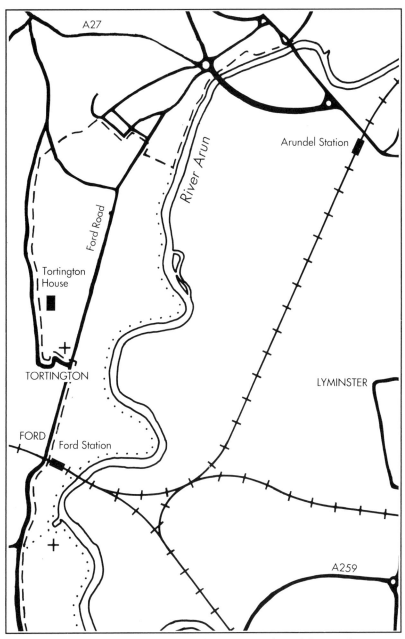

Route map, section 2: Littlehampton to Arundel, part B.
Scale 1: 25,000 - 2.5 inches to one mile.

The Bailiffscourt complex from the air.

Bailiffscourt chapel.

The house was built for Lord Moyne, who when minister resident in the Middle East was assassinated in November 1944 by members of the Zionist extremist organisation, Lehi, usually known as the Stern Gang. The assassination was part of a cycle of violence resulting from conflicting claims to what was known as Palestine which continues to this day. Lord Moyne's involvement with this problem dated from his appointment as Colonial Secretary in 1941. This post came after a distinguished record of public service. As Walter Guiness (he was a member of the brewing family) he became an MP in 1907 and was Minister of Agriculture in 1925. He was raised to the peerage in 1932 and thereafter was an inveterate traveller. The peace of the Sussex countryside provides a poignant contrast with the turbulence in distant lands which resulted in Lord Moyne's death.

Bailiffscourt is now a hotel, of rather an exclusive nature. Following the road north, one soon reaches, on the right, the Black Horse, an attractive public house which is in the village of Climping.

The Manor House at Bailiffscourt.

A short distance beyond the Black Horse there is a public footpath sign pointing to the right but that path no longer exists as it has been ploughed over. Some 300 yards further on another such sign indicates a tarmac path, and this is followed. The path veers to the right through fields. At St Mary's Church of England School an opportunity arises for the walker to return to Littlehampton by following a path which leads to the right and runs through fields before reaching the beach just to the east of Atherington. From that point the beach can be followed right back to Littlehampton or a footpath (mentioned earlier in relation to Cudlow) taken round the golf course; this emerges at the southern end of Rope Walk, close to where this chapter began. The route of the walk set out in the remainder of this chapter, however, goes past the school, then to the left along a short stretch of minor road, and crosses the (busy) A259 Littlehampton to Bognor road.

The tower of Climping Church.

Church Lane, opposite, which runs north from the A259, soon brings one to Climping Church, one of the finest of Sussex churches. The tower, the oldest part of the Church, had the capacity of providing a place of defence to the villagers, as well as a spiritual beacon. Probably built about 1170, it has a doorway which is a fine example of Norman dog-tooth work. The

The door to Climping Church.

tower may well have been attached originally to a wooden Saxon church. The interior of the present Church is early thirteenth century, perfectly proportioned, expressing spiritual faith without arrogance, ostentation or whimsy, essentially English but having the universality of the finest architecture. The furniture includes a thirteenth century Crusaders' chest; such chests were provided for offerings to enable poor knights to go on a crusade to the Holy Land. The visitors' book has quite a number of names from the United States and the Commonwealth, perhaps some of them people who first visited the church when stationed in England during the war and have since sought again its assertion of timeless values. It must be a matter of sadness that at the time of writing this book it was found necessary to keep the Church locked. Near the tower is the tomb of Lord Moyne, decorated with curious winged animals, improbable denizens of an English churchyard.

North of the Church is Ford Open Prison, which has recently had some new building. The route continues to the north, to a footpath with a stile,

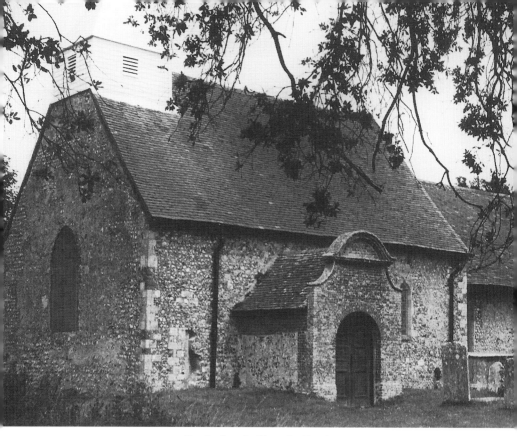

St. Andrew's Church, Ford.

opposite Ford Lane, which leads on the right to St. Andrew's Church. This Church is now closed, but it is possible to enter and explore the church-yard. The framework of the Church is eleventh century, but considerable work was done in succeeding centuries. The south porch was built in 1637 and has a Dutch gable.

North of the Church used to run the Portsmouth and Arundel Canal. This canal, in association with the Wey and Arun, provided a through route from London to Portsmouth when it was opened in 1823. However, the canals were uncompetitive in relation to the coastal route and, later, the railways; the Portsmouth and Arundel was a viable proposition for less than twenty years, although it was not officially abandoned until 1896. The entrance to the canal remains as the creek mentioned below. In the canal's brief heyday, there was a steam engine here to raise water from the Arun to supply the canal. Ridges in the land near the Church are thought to be of medieval origin. Building foundations were discovered when the canal was begun in 1818 and these may have represented the remains of the baronial mansion of the Bohun family.

The name "Ford" obviously suggests that the Arun was fordable at this point, and in 1927 evidence was discovered of a definite bar across the floor of the river. This was immediately below the junction with a stream known as the Binsted Brook. It has been persuasively argued by A. H. Allcroft in his *Waters of Arun* that the port of Arundel referred to in Domesday Book was at Ford, and certainly a Ford Dock existed at the time of Yeakell and Gardner's Map of 1788. It was about half a mile north of Ford Church.

From Ford, the route continues north along the road to Arundel as far as Tortington. It must be said that this route involves a walk of almost a mile along the verge of a busy road to reach Tortington, and further walking along - much less busy - roads before Arundel is gained. Those not inclined to embark on this venture may wish to stay with the path which continues round the back of the Church. After a short distance it reaches a small creek, into which the Binsted Brook, mentioned above, flows. The path passes houseboats on the right and a caravan site on the left before coming to the main stream of the Arun. The path can then be followed on to Arundel or back to Littlehampton.

Those who persist on the main road, past Ford Station, will be rewarded, like those who follow the river north, by fine distant views of Arundel, and should in addition find the hamlet of Tortington, on the left after a little under a mile, well worth a visit. There is an attractive Georgian house and, rather tucked away behind it and a farmyard, the Church of St. Mary Magdalene. The bell-turret gives the Church a considerable similarity to that at Ford. The most remarkable feature of the interior of the Church is the Norman chancel arch with somewhat bizarre faces sprouting leaves or feathers, alternating with long-beaked birds' heads. The Church is now in the care of the Redundant Churches Fund, which was set up in 1969 to preserve churches of historic or architectural interest which are no longer needed for regular worship.

Beyond the Church is Tortington House, which was built by Roger

St. Mary Magdalene's Church, Tortington.

Gratwicke, who died in 1596, and is commemorated by a brass plate in the Church. It was modernized in the early nineteenth century. Between 1922 and 1969 it was a private school for girls. After that, it was taken over by New England College, an educational institution based at Henniker, New Hampshire, as its "British Campus". The route continues north along a road which has little traffic and runs through pleasant, gently undulating, countryside. To the right is Priory Farm, the name of which marks the fact that it used to be the possession of Tortington Priory.

The buildings of this Priory, founded before 1180, once covered eight acres. The Priory, which was linked with that at Hardham described in Chapter 7, did not have an entirely unchequered history. In 1376 Pope Gregory XI stated in a bull that the Prior John Palmere, careless not only of propriety, but of his own good name, was living dissolutely outside the monastery, and orders were given for his trial and deposition if guilty.

The road runs under high voltage wires and enters a wood. The route continues along the road past a metal barred gate on the right and after about 200 yards follows a path to the right (opposite a stile with a fence to the left) which crosses another narrow road and leads, rather surprisingly perhaps after such rural seclusion, into a trim housing estate, at Dalloway Road. The route turns right, to reach Stewards Rise; at the end of that road it turns left into Priory Road then shortly, at a mini-roundabout, right down Maxwell Road to the Climping - Arundel road.

A short walk to the right along this road brings one to a path on the left, marked as a public footpath between high hedges, leading back to the Arun. The route now follows the path left along the river towards Arundel.

As one walks towards the town there is a panorama; on the right, on the far bank, is the South Marshes windmill built in 1840, sadly without its sails, but in residential use. The Castle, Parish Church and Cathedral rise above an attractively jumbled roof-line. The path along the river runs under a severely functional bridge carrying the by-pass, then continues straight ahead. A stonemason's yard is passed on the left, a fence to the right; the path then runs into Tarrant Street. A short walk to the right along this Street brings one to the King's Arms on the left; the route turns to the right down Arun Street, which has cottages in various materials including flint. At the end of Arun Street is a garden with lavender and other bushes, overlooking the river. The route continues alongside the river through a short footpath and then River Road (with an old shipyard building to the left) to the bottom of the High Street. The walker may well want to seek refreshment in Arundel at this point, and this seems a suitable point at which to sketch in an outline - it can be no more - of the history of the Earls of Arundel and Dukes of Norfolk, of the Castle and of Arundel itself, before suggesting an itinerary around the town.

CHAPTER 4. The Earls of Arundel and Dukes of Norfolk

The Castle's domination of the Arundel skyline is an apt symbol of the rôle which it has played in the life of the town for almost a thousand years. In the relaxed, still slightly feudal, atmosphere of modern Arundel it is easy to imagine Earls of Arundel, masters of all that they surveyed, passing on from generation to generation a peaceful position of lordship over the town and its surroundings. In reality, however, the Earldom of Arundel and the Dukedom of Norfolk had for several centuries a record of remarkable turbulence and violence, close to the heart of national political events.

The Earldom, along with that of Shrewsbury, was granted by William the Conqueror to one of his leading Norman nobles, Roger de Montgomery. The first upheaval came after William's death in 1087. He had left Normandy to his eldest son, Robert, and England to William Rufus, the second. Roger de Montgomery, basing himself on Shrewsbury and in association with other Welsh border barons, joined in an unsuccessful rebellion in support of Robert's claim to the English throne. In this instance, backing the wrong side had no disastrous consequences, and Roger returned to royal favour. Roger arranged for the division of his lands after his death, his younger son Hugh taking the English possessions. Hugh, like his father, rebelled against William Rufus; and died fighting in Anglesey. His elder brother, Robert of Bellême, who already owned the family estates in Normandy, now took over the English ones also, and became the third Earl.

Robert de Bellême continued the family tradition of rebellion by taking up arms against Henry I in the interests of Robert Duke of Normandy. His castles, including Arundel, were taken, and he was banished to Normandy, where he conducted a reign of terror. Robert de Bellême's destabilising effect on Normandy was a factor in encouraging Henry I to invade it. All his property was confiscated to the Crown following the defeat of the Duke of Normandy's forces (and capture of the Duke himself) at the Battle of Tinchebrai in 1106; so ended the Montgomery connection with Arundel. Robert of Bellême died in captivity at Wareham in Dorset in 1118 and his son William succeeded to his father's inheritance in Normandy.

Henry I left Arundel to his widow, Queen Adeliza, who married William de Albini, who became the fourth Earl, the title being conveyed to him by his wife. We known little of William's background, although his father had the title of chief butler to the King. His rise must have been a dizzy one. The change of family in the Earldom didn't bring any relief from political strife. William de Albini supported Matilda, Henry I's daughter and Adzilla's step-daughter, against King Stephen. Matilda arrived at Arundel in 1139 to assert her claim to the throne, and was besieged there by Stephen, who decided to let her escape to the west of England. William then changed his allegiance and supported Stephen, subsequently helping to bring about good relations between Stephen and Henry of Anjou, Matilda's son, who, when he became king as Henry II, rewarded William with the Earldom of Sussex.

From this point, the Earldom of Arundel entered calmer waters for a while, the line continuing without untoward interruption until the eighth Earl died without issue in 1263. His property was divided, and he was succeeded at Arundel by his nephew John Fitzalan, although doubts have been expressed as to whether John and his son of the same name actually held the Earldom, introducing one of a number of elements of potential confusion into the numbering of the Earls. The second John's son Richard, who succeeded in 1272, can be regarded as the ninth Earl.

Richard took part in Edward I's wars. His son Edmund, tenth Earl, was caught up in the civil strife which characterised the reign of Edward II, and was beheaded at Hereford in 1326, having fallen foul of Queen Isabella and her lover Roger Mortimore. Under an Act of Attainder (an Act of Parliament registering conviction for treason and declaring all property forfeit to the Crown) Arundel was granted to the Earl of Kent, but it was restored to Richard the eleventh Earl, who served in Scottish wars, then won a naval victory over the French at the Battle of Sluys in 1340, subsequently fighting at Crécy in 1346 and at the siege of Calais, which took place in 1346 - 1347.

After Richard's death in 1376, his son, also called Richard, succeeded as twelfth Earl. Reference is made in subsequent chapters to the twelfth Earl's noteworthy contribution to Arundel through the foundation of the Maison Dieu and of Arundel College, in association with which he rebuilt the Parish Church of St. Nicholas. Nationally, he was active in both the military and naval spheres, becoming Admiral of England. Unhappily, he fell victim to the political intrigues which beset the reign of Richard II, and was executed for treason. This did not prevent him from being revered for his good works.

Richard's son Thomas restored the family fortunes by successfully plotting, along with his uncle the Archbishop of Canterbury, to replace Richard II with Henry Bolingbroke. After Richard's deposition, Archbishop Arundel crowned Henry in Westminster as Henry IV, and Thomas was restored to his father's position at Arundel. After Henry IV died, Thomas went on to serve Henry V with distinction, in offices which included that of Lord High Treasurer. He died in 1415 of dysentry contracted at the siege of Harfleur.

Thomas was succeeded by his great-nephew John, a soldier, whose son the fifteenth Earl, also called John, won military glory in the Hundred Years' War. He died in 1435 and was succeeded by his son Humphrey who died in childhood, with the title passing to his uncle William, who successfully navigated the stormy waters of the Wars of Roses and died at the Castle in 1487.

William was succeeded by his son Thomas and grandson William, the latter a close friend of Henry VIII. William's son Henry, who succeeded in 1544 as the twentieth Earl, was a suitor of Elizabeth I, but is described by J. E. Neale in his famous biography of the Queen as "rather silly and loutish". He was later associated, along with the Duke of Norfolk, in the Ridolfi Plot, to which further reference is made below. He avoided trouble sufficiently, however, to die at his London home, Arundel House, in 1580.

It is at this point that the Dukedom of Norfolk comes into the story of Arundel. Henry's son of the same name died in 1556 at Brussels as a result of a fever caught while on an embassy to the King of Bohemia, and his daughter Mary became his heiress. She married, in the year of her brother Henry's death, Thomas the fourth (Howard) Duke of Norfolk, whose career is summarised below, but sadly died in the following year soon after giving birth to her son Philip, who in due course became the first Howard to hold the Earldom of Arundel. The Howard family was one of the greatest in England. It was set on its upward path in the thirteenth century by Sir William Howard, a lawyer who became Chief Justice of the Common Pleas. The family advanced through military distinction and favourable marriages, a notable step being the marriage in about 1420 of Sir Robert Howard to Lady Margaret Mowbray, elder daughter of Thomas Mowbray, Duke of Norfolk and Earl Marshal of England. The lack of male heirs to the Mowbrays put the Howards into the line of succession to the Dukedom of Norfolk. Sir John Howard, Robert's son and a strong supporter of Richard III, received the Dukedom in 1483, and died at the Battle of Bosworth in 1485. His son Thomas also fought on the losing side at Bosworth, but he restored the family name and became a leading statesman and military figure of Henry VIII's reign, leading the English army to victory over the Scots at the Battle of Flodden in 1513.

Thomas was succeeded by his son the third Duke, also called Thomas, two of whose nieces, Anne Boleyn and Katherine Howard, were married to Henry VIII and later executed. Thomas, having advanced them as part of his political plans, did nothing to save them. Eventually Thomas himself fell from favour with Henry VIII, partly through the behaviour of his brilliant but headstrong son the Earl of Surrey, who among his other accomplishments was a poet whose work has retained its appeal across the centuries. Surrey was executed on the flimsiest of charges; Thomas was saved because Henry VIII died just before his execution was due to take place.

The fourth Duke - another Thomas - succeeded his grandfather in 1554, and settled naturally into a leading rôle in the kingdom. Thomas was related to Elizabeth I, was the only Duke in the country, had great estates and also many accomplishments including interests in scholarship and in architecture. Unhappily, the tragic fate which so often stalked the family struck Thomas in full measure.

It was the misfortunes of private life which paved the way to Thomas's political disaster. Three times Thomas became a widower, and it was his unmarried status which led to a plan in which his ambition overreached itself, to marry Mary Queen of Scots. Elizabeth was mistrustful, and Thomas became enmeshed in an intrigue known as the Ridolfi Plot. Ridolfi was a Florentine banker whose plans involved an invasion of England by the Duke of Alva, the Spanish Governor of the Netherlands, in support of a rising designed to put Mary Queen of Scots on the throne instead of Elizabeth. Perhaps one should say his purported plans, as it has been suggested that he was a double agent. Many circumstances of the plot remain obscure, and the atmosphere of conspiracy and double-crosses would make a suitable theme for John le Carré. The outcome was the Duke's trial for treason, his attainder, and execution in 1572, with the confiscation of the family estates. These included Arundel Castle and the Fitzalan estates in Sussex, linked with those of the Howards as a result of Thomas's first marriage, mentioned above, to Lady Mary Fitzalan, the daughter of the twentieth Earl of Arundel. Although the Howard family was to show constant resilience right down to the present day, the downfall of the fourth Duke marked the end of an era; never again would the family fully return to its splendid - and dangerous - position at the heart of the nation's political affairs.

Thomas's son Philip is now perhaps the best remembered of all the Howards. He had inherited the Earldom of Arundel through his mother, and his father's disgrace did not initially affect his career at Elizabeth's court. His life took a new turn, however, on his conversion to Roman Catholicism - his father, unusually in the family, had been a Protestant. It is not easy, even now, to regard the religious controversies of that time in a dispassionate light. On the one hand, there is no question about the bravery and sincerity of the Roman Catholic priests and laymen who maintained their faith in the face of persecution. On the other hand, Pope Pius V had in his bull *Regnans in Excelsis*, issued in 1570, proclaimed Elizabeth's deposition and absolved Englishmen from their oath of allegiance to her. It is hardly surprising, therefore, that Elizabeth and her government regarded the Roman Catholic faith as a threat to what we would call national security.

It was in this atmosphere that Philip decided to flee the country. He was intercepted, arraigned before the Star Chamber, committed to the Tower, and, after tension had been increased by the Spanish Armada, tried for

44

treason. In spite of the deficiencies in evidence he was found guilty, condemned to death, and returned to the Tower. Elizabeth did not sign the death warrant but Philip was not told that, and his imprisonment in the Tower - grim in any circumstances - was made worse by the fact that he believed that he might at any time face execution. In 1595, shortly before he died, he asked to see his wife and children, but Elizabeth would not allow him to do this unless he renounced his faith, which he refused to do. Philip was canonized by Pope Paul VI in 1970.

It is beyond the scope of this book to describe the general history of the members of the Howard family, such as Lord Howard of Effingham, who commanded the English fleet against the Armada; this narrative must confine itself to tracing briefly the story of the Earls of Arundel and Dukes of Norfolk. Philip's only son Thomas was restored to the Earldom of Arundel by James I in 1604. Known as the "Collector Earl", Thomas was a patron of the arts and took a close interest in the history of the Howards. He had a somewhat chequered political career, but by the 1630s had achieved a position of dignity in the life of the nation which, if it did not fully match the status of some of his ancestors, was by no means unworthy of the family tradition. He was not, however, to be granted a tranquil old age, for he lived to know England engulfed in Civil War and Arundel Castle a centre of battle. At least he was not to see this happen with his own eyes, for his last years were spent in Italy.

Thomas's son Henry fought on the Royalist side in the Civil War, but generally did little to add to the distinction of the family's name. Henry's eldest son Thomas's mental balance was adversely affected by illness, but this did not prevent the Dukedom being restored to him during the reign of Charles II. The next eldest son, another Henry, conducted the affairs of the Dukedom and eventually succeeded to it, but he was a victim of the religious tensions of the time, and spent an increasing amount of his life at his house near Bruges.

Henry's son - another Henry - succeeded his father as the seventh Duke. A pragmatic man, he did a great deal to consolidate the Howard position. Nevertheless, he did not exactly have a quiet life; with him, the often tragic character of the family history turned to farce; he initiated a divorce case, which was robustly defended by his wife, and the hearings before the

House of Lords became something of a public entertainment.

Henry died in 1700, and was succeeded by his nephew Thomas, a person of strong religious views in the Catholic tradition usually - although as we have already seen not universally - adhered to by the Howards. Although he did not play a prominent rôle in politics, he was accused of involvement in a Jacobite plot and, like a number of his predecessors, was imprisoned in the Tower. Henry thereafter concentrated on looking after his estates, which included undertaking some work at Arundel Castle, although he visited the Castle rarely.

This concentration on family estates was continued by Thomas's son Edward, the ninth Duke, who succeeded in 1732. Edward's life was one of placid consolidation of the family position, in keeping with that calming of the more extreme political and religious passions which marked the course of the eighteenth century. On his death in 1777, the Dukedom passed to Charles, the grandson of a brother of Thomas and Henry, the fifth and sixth Dukes. Charles, a somewhat reclusive man, seems to have been rather overawed by his rôle as the tenth Duke, but his son, also called Charles, who succeeded him in 1786, was a hard-living, hard-drinking Whig, who used Arundel Castle for entertaining. His work on the Castle and the grounds is outlined in the following chapter. Charles's enjoyment of his traditional ducal rôle, and his radicalism, found expression in a dinner and entertainment he put on at Arundel in June 1815 to celebrate the six hundredth anniversary of the signing of the Magna Carta. It was all some way from the austere pieties of one strand in the Howard tradition; but the religious element in that tradition was far from exhausted.

Charles had no direct heir, and on his death later in 1815 the Dukedom passed to Bernard, great-grandson of another brother of the fifth and sixth Dukes. Bernard, the twelfth Duke, was a man of strong Roman Catholic views and a leading advocate of Catholic Emancipation, which he saw as enabling members of his faith to make a full contribution to the mainstream of English life. He had the satisfaction of being able, under the terms of the 1829 Emancipation Act, to take his seat in the House of Lords.

Bernard's son Henry succeeded as thirteenth Duke in 1842; a man very conscious of the dignity of his position. In his time Queen Victoria and Prince Albert visited Arundel Castle, a successful social event. His chaplain, Canon Tierney, was the author of *The History and Antiquities of the Castle and Town of Arundel* which, along with G. W. Eustace's *Arundel Borough and Castle*, remains a valuable source for Arundel history. Henry died in 1860.

Henry's son, of the same name, succeeded as fourteenth Duke. A very devout man, he was more influenced than his predecessors by the continental tradition of Roman Catholicism. He devoted much of his income to religious and charitable causes. He held the Dukedom for only four years, dying in 1860. His son - another Henry - lived until 1917, a tenure of the Dukedom which provides a sort of bridge from the historic past into a world we can to some extent recognise as similar to our own. The photographic record, in itself, can give us a greater sense of knowledge of the man and his times than is available in relation to the earlier Dukes.

Nevertheless, the social and economic context of the Duke's life was very different from that which obtains today, and the Duke's cast of mind was also one scarcely familiar now. He carried on his father's tradition of devoting substantial sums of money to good works, and he had a particular interest in the commissioning of buildings, both religious and secular, the evidence of which is inescapable in Arundel. He built a new Roman Catholic Church for Arundel, the Church of St. Philip Neri, now the Cathedral of Our Lady and St. Philip Howard. As will be seen in Chapter 7, the current appearance of the Castle owes much to him.

On the national scene, Henry as the leading Roman Catholic layman in the country had an active involvement in matters related to his faith, including relations with the Vatican. Among other examples of his public service he held the office of Postmaster General, and his interests extended to local government, not only in Sussex but in London, where he was a member of the London County Council and the first Lord Mayor of Westminster.

Henry's son Bernard brings the Dukedom fully into the modern world. He maintained the family tradition of adaptation to the interests of the age; for if at one time our national preoccupation had been war, high politics,

Henry Fitzalan-Howard, fifteenth Duke of Norfolk, 1890.

or religion, what could be more English in the second half of the twentieth century than devotion to cricket? In addition to discharging the usual ceremonial duties of a Duke of Norfolk, including those of the hereditary position of Earl Marshal, Bernard was President of MCC and manager of the English cricket team on its tour of Australia and New Zealand in 1962-63.

Bernard died in 1975 and was succeeded by Miles, the seventeenth and current Duke, the great-grandson of Edward, brother of the fourteenth Duke. Miles was a professional soldier, and has continued what has become the traditional rôle of the Dukes of Norfolk in the life of the Roman Catholic Church and the nation.

CHAPTER 5. Arundel Castle and Priory

It is not the intention of this chapter to attempt to duplicate the detailed descriptions in the guide book on sale at the Castle, but instead to provide historical background on the Castle, the Fitzalan Chapel and Arundel Priory especially as they have reflected the personalities and circumstances of Earls of Arundel and Dukes of Norfolk whose lives have been outlined in the previous chapter.

Although a Saxon origin has been claimed for the Castle, firm knowledge starts with Roger de Montgomery. The broad plan of the Castle derives from his time; the central fortified mound (motte) with upper and lower courtyards (baileys) protected by a curtain wall. The fact that there is no public admission to part of the upper bailey (now known as the Tilting Yard) may tend to obscure the overall plan of the Castle in the mind of the visitor.

The only building which survives from Roger de Montgomery's time is the Gatehouse. Perhaps a little confusingly, this is not the first building by which one enters the Castle - that is the Barbican, built by Richard, the ninth Earl, as part of his strengthening of defences of Castle and town which also included the building of the town wall - but is a continuation of it, very clearly identified however by the Inner Gateway. Only the lower part of the Gatehouse is as Roger de Montgomery left it, the upper part having been rebuilt by Richard. Between Roger de Montgomery and Richard, the major builder at the Castle was William de Albini, who was responsible for the Keep, for work to the curtain wall and for the Bevis Tower. William's wish to strengthen the Castle was very understandable given the political instability of his time, as indicated in Chapter 4.

A phase in the life of the Castle of which there is now little evidence - save for marks of cannon balls on the Barbican walls - is the Civil War siege of December 1643/January 1644 to which reference is made in the following chapter. In October 1649 the Council of State of the new Commonwealth

*Arundel Castle: a view of the whole complex, looking towards the river (south is, therefore, at the **top** of this photo). The various parts of the complex show up very clearly from this viewpoint.*

Government ordered the demolition of most of the Castle. Surprising as it may now seem, the Castle remained in a ruinous condition until about 1720, when Thomas, the sixth Duke, undertook substantial restoration with a view to establishing the Castle once again as the primary seat of his family.

The restoration went considerably further under Charles, the eleventh Duke, whose substantial rebuilding included a Barons' Hall and Chapel, predecessors of those we now see. It was for his benefit that Hiorne's Tower was built as an example of the style of restoration which might be used. Charles consolidated the general position of the Castle in 1803 by diverting the London Road at the top of the High Street in a more westerly direction and by erecting a wall on the north side of that Road, protecting the privacy of the grounds. He also expanded the Castle land to the north, forming the Castle Park as it now exists.

It is, however, to Henry the fifteenth Duke that we owe the Castle in its present form. His building programme started in the late 1870s. The east wing was extended to the north, beyond the library, to provide a suite of private rooms, and the south and west wings were reconstructed. The work of rebuilding included the Barons' Hall and the Chapel, the work, as already mentioned, of Charles the eleventh Duke. The architect of the Chapel - as of much of Duke Henry's work - was Alban Buckler.

Whether Duke Henry was well advised to embark on such an extensive reconstruction of the work of Duke Charles is very much a matter of opinion. His accurate restoration of the surviving medieval elements of the Castle and of the Fitzalan Chapel are open to much less question.

The early history of the Fitzalan Chapel is outlined below, in the context of Arundel Priory. The Chapel had been damaged and used as a stable by Parliamentary troops during the Civil War, and by the eighteenth century was in a very poor condition. The action authorised by Duke Charles to remedy this situation was most unfortunate. The partly-decayed roof timbers were cut through and allowed to fall into the Chapel, where they did a great deal of damage to stalls and tombs, and an anachronistic slate roof was installed.

Duke Henry's restoration was on more authentic lines, and gave us the Fitzalan Chapel as we now see it, with its remarkable collection of tombs of Earls of Arundel and Dukes of Norfolk prompting thoughts both of transience and permanence. Were Philip Larkin, in his poem "An Arundel Tomb", to have been writing about this place, he could have been said to have caught the atmosphere with remarkable accuracy and sympathy. He writes of the tomb of an Earl of Arundel and his wife whose effigies hold hands, the emotions of life communicated to us through the sculptor's art. In his words, the effigies

Persisted, linked, through lengths and breadths
Of time. Snow fell, undated. Light
Each summer thronged the glass. A bright
Litter of birdcalls strewed the same
Bone-riddled ground . . . .

Perhaps a little disappointingly, however, the tomb concerned was located not in this Chapel but in Chichester Cathedral.

The Chapel was originally part of Arundel College, the other surviving elements of which constitute Arundel Priory, which can be seen to good advantage from the London Road and to which reference is made in Chapter 7. The College, founded in 1380 by Richard the twelfth Earl, replaced the Benedictine Priory of St. Nicholas endowed by Roger the first Earl, which had fallen on hard times. The Priory buildings were demolished as was the old Parish Church. The College was built around a quadrangle, on the north side of which was the Chapel, now the Fitzalan Chapel. Although the sharpness of the distinction between the Fitzalan Chapel and the Parish Church of which it appears to be a part derives, as explained in Chapter 7, from the Reformation, the function of the Chapel was always distinct from that of the Church, and part of the Chapel's rôle was, from the beginning, that of a memorial to the Fitzalan family. The Chapel was designed by William de Wynford, notable as master mason of New College Oxford and Winchester Cathedral.

In 1544 Arundel College was suppressed by Henry VIII and the buildings, except for the Chapel and the Master's Lodgings, were partly demolished and allowed to fall into ruin. Charles the eleventh Duke, other aspects of whose building activities have already been described in this chapter, put in hand the repair of what college buildings survived. As part of the restoration, an Oratory was provided: this is now the theatre mentioned in Chapter 7. The College buildings became a convent in the time of Henry the fourteenth Duke, and provided accommodation for a school and, after the buildings ceased to be used as a convent, a children's home; they now house almshouses run under the auspices of the Order of St. John.

A view of Arundel Castle (south front) from the river.

CHAPTER 6. History of Arundel

Aspects of Arundel history have been brought out in the previous two chapters; further aspects will appear in the following one. It is the purpose of this chapter to provide a historical summary, concentrating mainly on the town rather than the Castle, which will help, so to speak, to enable pieces of the jigsaw to be fitted together.

The first inhabitants of what we now call Arundel who have left us evidence of their presence are the Belgic people who are thought to have built what is known as the War Dyke (although the function of this earthwork is disputed) which runs from the Arun west of North Stoke to Whiteways Plantation west of the A284, as well as the rampart mentioned on the next page. A Belgic settlement in Arundel Park known as Shepherd's Garden has been excavated. The discovery of the remains of a Roman villa by the Arun, at the western end of Tarrant Street, provided evidence of the next phase of Arundel's existence.

Little is known of Saxon Arundel; a reference to the manor appears in the will of Alfred the Great (901) and the Domesday Book tells us that in the time of Edward the Confessor there were, among other features, a port and as mentioned in Chapter 7 an early version of the Church of St. Nicholas. The picture becomes much clearer, however, after the Norman Conquest. Roger de Montgomery not only built the Castle but also established Arundel as a Borough, with rights of self-government, in 1086.

The relationship between Castle and town has remained, naturally enough, a very close one from those early days until now. Adeliza, the wife of the fourth Earl, for example provided a new bridge across the Arun and an associated causeway across adjacent marshy land. Richard, the ninth Earl, protected the town by building a wall, which ran west of the edge of the Castle moat near the Bevis Tower to St. Mary's Gate north-west of St. Nicholas's Church, then across the line now taken by the London Road and down what is now called Mount Pleasant (formerly Poorhouse Hill).

However pervasive the influence of the Castle, the town flourished in its own right, with its dignitaries led by the Mayor, its right to hold a market, and from 1295 until the Reform Bill of 1832 its sending of two Members of Parliament to Westminster. The town's concerns were in no way of such significance to the nation as the activities of the Earls of Arundel and Dukes of Norfolk, but Arundel was thrust rudely onto the national stage during the Civil War.

At the end of 1642, with the Civil War only a few months old, Sir William Waller, commander of the parliamentary forces south of the Thames, arrived at Arundel on his way to Chichester. The Castle was lightly held by Henry, son of Thomas the "Collector Earl"; Waller seized it with a force of 36 men, not one of whom was killed. The ease with which the Castle was taken possibly indicates support for the parliamentary side among the townspeople.

A year later, there was a change of fortune when Lord Hopton, whose advance across the Weald had been assisted by hard frost, took the town on behalf of the King; the odds against the parliamentary garrison of the Castle were so great that the Castle was surrendered. Within less than two weeks, however, Waller, helped by the same weather conditions which had previously aided Hopton, had returned to Arundel, and the royalist besiegers became the besieged. Sir Edward Ford, the commander of the royalist garrison, employed as a first line of defence the Belgic earth rampart and its extension described in Chapter 7, but this was soon forced and the royalists confined to the Castle. Some of the residents of Arundel took refuge in St. Nicholas's Church; they surrendered when the Parliamentary forces threatened to burn them out. The parliamentarians subsequently used the tower of St. Nicholas's Church as a gun platform. The Castle sustained for seventeen days, a siege which had its civilised moments - during a parley the defenders said that they desired "sack, tobacco, cards and dice". In order to stop the Castle's water supply, Swanbourne Lake was drained. The problems of defending the Castle were compounded by differences among the garrison's commanding officers. Following the failure of an attempt at relief by Hopton the situation of the garrison was clearly hopeless, and the royalists surrendered on 6 January 1644; some thousand prisoners were taken. Waller repaired Arundel's defences before he left the town. In October 1649, after the end of the English Civil War, most of the Castle was demolished, as mentioned in Chapter 5. In 1659, ten years after the decision to demolish most of the Castle, demolition of the town wall was ordered.

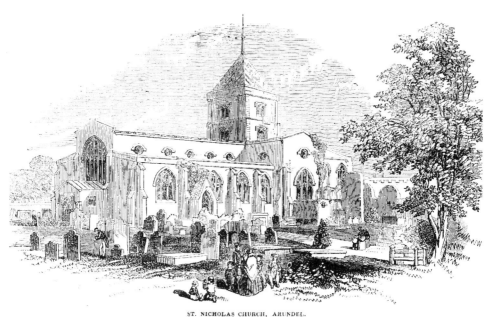

ST. NICHOLAS CHURCH, ARUNDEL.

St. Nicholas's Church, Arundel, in 1865.

The restoration of Charles II, and with him of the Church of England, in 1660 soon brought with it political changes to the town. Under the Corporation Act, as clarified by the Act of Conformity of 1662, the Mayor and Corporation were required to take communion according to the rites of the Church of England, which as Presbyterians they refused to do. They were replaced by a new, Anglican, Mayor and Corporation.

After the upheavals of the seventeenth century, Arundel's concerns were once again mainly with local rather than national matters. In 1724 the wooden bridge over the Arun was replaced by a stone one, which lasted until the present bridge was built in 1935. In 1773 buildings were demolished to form the Market Square at the bottom of the High Street. In 1785, an Act of Parliament "For the better Paving, Cleansing and Lighting the Streets, Lanes, Ways and Passages within the Borough of

Arundel, in the County of Sussex; and for removing and preventing Incroachments, Obstructions and Annoyances there in" marked a further stage in "tidying up" the town. Charles Howard, subsequently the eleventh Duke of Norfolk, and the Mayor and Burgesses of the town were appointed as Commissioners to administer the provisions of the Act, which included a ban on letting off fireworks in the street. The Act specified that the Commissioners should hold their first meeting at the Norfolk Arms, so they no doubt embarked on their duties with a degree of conviviality.

In the early nineteenth century Arundel reached what was perhaps the height of its prosperity. The population rose from 2,188 in 1811 to 2,803 in 1831. Trade increased because of the improved navigability of the Arun arising from the harbour improvements at Littlehampton in 1798, fine new houses were built, a theatre opened, and Arundel became socially fashionable. A new town hall - at the east end of Maltravers Street - was completed about 1836. However, the economic significance of Arundel was starting to diminish with slackening of trade, a tendency which continued in spite of the coming of the railway in 1863.

As the nineteenth century progressed, however, it saw a remarkable programme of works by the Dukes of Norfolk. The story of the Castle at that time has been given in Chapter 5; that of what was then the Church of St. Philip Neri is set out in Chapter 7; the rebuilt Castle and what is now the Cathedral of Our Lady and St. Philip Howard represent only the most prominent of Ducal initiatives, others including the laying out of Mill Road and the building of the mock-Tudor post office when the fifteenth Duke was Postmaster General.

During the twentieth century, the pattern of economic activity in Arundel has changed markedly, with a decline in manufacturing and the disappearance of the once-important port, and a diminished rôle for agriculture; tourism has become increasingly important, and many residents now earn a living outside the town. Arundel continues to flourish, showing at the time when this book was written no signs of the adverse economic conditions evident in other parts of Sussex, as elsewhere in the country. One can envisage it as very little changed as it moves into the twenty-first century.

CHAPTER 7. Walk around Arundel

Distance: *About three and a half miles.*

Walking Conditions: *Roads; paths, mostly firm, but includes the climbing*
                           of a path which is slippery in wet weather.

Station: *Arundel.*

Arundel Bridge, at the north end of which this walk starts, replaced in 1935, as mentioned in Chapter 6, a bridge which was built in 1724, itself the successor of previous bridges going back to Norman times. Nearby is a ruined monastic building which for more than two hundred years was identified as the Maison Dieu founded by Richard, the fourteenth Earl of Arundel. It has now however been convincingly demonstrated by Dr. Timothy Hudson, West Sussex editor of the *Victoria History of the Counties of England,* that the ruins are in fact those of the south range of a thirteenth century Dominican Friary; unfortunately it is not now possible to trace on the ground the full scale of the Friary. Just beyond the Friary, to the left, is the entrance to the Castle, the subject of the previous chapter.

The route continues along Mill Road, a tree-lined avenue which was funded by Henry, the fifteenth Duke of Norfolk, and opened in 1892. The road crosses a bridge at the outfall from Swanbourne Lake. From the bridge can be seen the former Arundel Castle Dairy building which replaced the watermill which gave the road its name and which is thought to have been on the site of the one recorded in the Domesday Book as having belonged to Earl Roger. Near the old Dairy building is Swanbourne Lodge, one of the Castle Lodges, now a tea house. Swanbourne Lake itself is used for boating; almost surrounded as it is by steeply rising ground, it presents an idyllic picture.

A short distance beyond Swanbourne Lake, on the right, is the Wildfowl

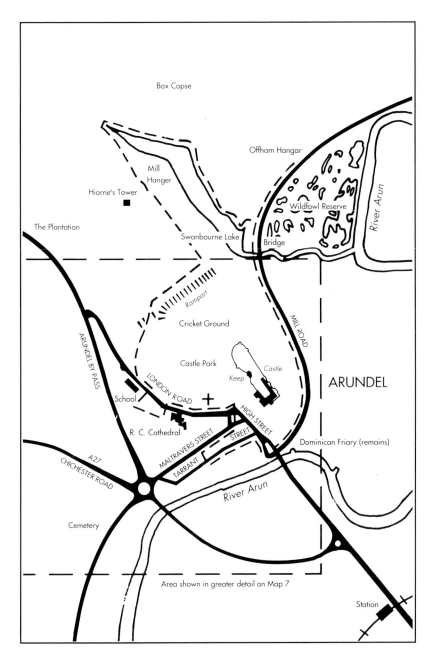

Arundel and its environs. Scale 1:17,500 - 3.5 inches to one mile.

Trust's Arundel Reserve, with the steep Offham Hanger (a hanger being a wood on a hillside) rising to the left. The Wildfowl Trust, whose first and best known reserve is that at Slimbridge in Gloucestershire, aims to provide areas where the public can see a wide variety of waterfowl, both native species and those from far afield. The Reserve consists of a complex of lakes and ponds with surrounding vegetation, and certainly achieves the Trust's objectives, although unhappily it has been the subject of something of an "invasion" by Canada Geese, which tend to harass the other birds. While this reserve may lack the wide horizons of Slimbridge, it has an attractive setting and that and the variety of ducks and geese which are to be found make it well worth a visit.

From the Reserve, the route returns to Swanbourne Lodge and Lake. Here it is of course possible to return to Arundel via Mill Road, but the recommended route takes the path on the north side of Swanbourne Lake past the Lodge and a refreshment kiosk. It is possible to walk along the south of the lake, but that path is muddy after rain - the northern path is firmer.

At the far end of the lake the path divides and the left fork is taken round the end of the lake. On the right there is a fence ascending the ridge on which Arundel Castle stands, and the route follows an (unmarked) path alongside this fence. The path is rather steep, but the views compensate for the effort involved in climbing. Towards the summit of the ridge, the Arun may be seen winding towards Burpham. As the plateau at the top of the ridge is reached, Hiorne's Tower comes into view. This was built in 1790 by Francis Hiorne for the eleventh Duke, as described in Chapter 5. The path curves to the left and then continues straight on until a fence is reached. Beyond this may be seen a substantial earth rampart (now covered by nettles and other vegetation) regarded as the work of the Belgic people who built the War Dyke to the north. The route continues to the right along a path which meets a roadway by Park Lodge - the entrance to the cricket ground on which the opening match of each overseas team's tour is played against the Duchess of Norfolk's XI. It follows the road past a forge and through a continuation of the rampart to which the route has been running parallel. It is thought that this section of earthwork is not contemporary with the rest, but may date from 1643, when the royalists were defending Arundel, as described in Chapter 6; the

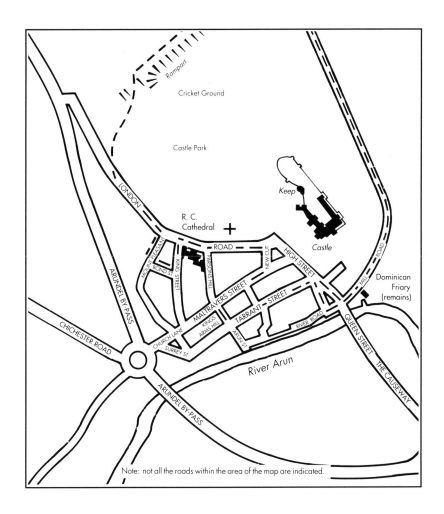

Town map of Arundel. Scale 1:15,840 - 4 inches to one mile.

original rampart turns more sharply south behind Park Lodge. The route continues to the main (London) Road, turns left and passes St. Philip's Roman Catholic Primary School and the Roman Catholic Cemetery. The St. Mary's Gate Inn on the right is a reminder of the existence of the Mary Gate, where the London Road used to pass through the town walls. The Gate, the first conclusive reference to which was in 1343, had a Chapel as its top floor - the Chapel of Blessed Mary Over the Gate. This Chapel was destroyed during the Civil War, and when Charles, the eleventh Duke of Norfolk, diverted the London Road (as mentioned in Chapter 5), the Mary Gate, situated north-west of St. Nicholas' Church, was incorporated into the Castle grounds. The eleventh Duke restored a top floor to the Gate, which remains now as he rebuilt it. Just before the Inn, the route turns right down Mount Pleasant (formerly the line of the town wall, as indicated in Chapter 6), and then follows Bond Street, the first turning to the left. Both roads have attractive early nineteenth century flint terraces. Bond Street leads into King Street; the route turns left here, to the Roman Catholic Cathedral of Our Lady and St. Philip Howard, built as the Church of St. Philip Neri under the patronage of Henry the fifteenth Duke in 1870-73. The architect was Joseph Hansom the founder of the *Builder* magazine and inventor of the Hansom cab. George Myers was the builder. Hansom's original designs showed greater elaboration than the building we now see, which reflects the Duke's own views. There was an intention to have a spire over the north-west porch but the foundations were not thought strong enough to carry it. As with the fifteenth Duke's rebuilding at the castle, there is room for debate as to how successful the nineteenth century use of medieval architectural idiom proved to be in the attempt to recreate the spirit of past times. When the Roman Catholic Diocese of Arundel and Brighton was established in 1965 the Church became a Cathedral, its new name including a commemoration of St. Philip Howard, to whom reference is made in Chapter 4.

On the opposite side of London Road, a little further on is St. Nicholas's Church. The history of this Church is closely involved with that of Arundel Castle and Priory, and that relationship is brought out in Chapter 5.

There was originally a Saxon Church of St. Nicholas on this site, which was recorded in the Domesday Book. After the Conquest this Church appears to have been subject to enlargement or rebuilding, and the resulting Norman Church was itself demolished, and the current building erected, by Richard the twelfth Earl in association with his foundation of Arundel College. The design of that part of the building which is now the Parish Church was the responsibility of Henry Yevele, the master mason whose best known work is the naves of Canterbury Cathedral and Westminster Abbey.

After the suppression of Arundel College in 1544 mentioned in Chapter 5, the chancel of the Church, which was also the Chapel of the College, was sold along with the rest of the College by Henry VIII to Henry the twentieth Earl of Arundel, to whom reference is made in Chapter 4, for £1,000. The subsequent history of the Chapel is outlined in Chapter 5; as a private Roman Catholic Chapel, it now had a different denominational identity from the Anglican Parish Church. The iron grille which already separated the Church from its Chapel now had more profound symbolic significance; the grille remained locked for centuries, the keys in the possession of the Earls of Arundel/Dukes of Norfolk.

During the nineteenth century restoration of the Church was undertaken by Sir Gilbert Scott, and in 1976 work took place to bring its layout more in line with current thinking. In 1977 the iron grille was opened and the Church used for a single service for the first time since the Reformation.

At the north-west corner of the churchyard are sections of wall which incorporate stonework which has now been identified as almost certainly the remains of the Maison Dieu. This was founded by Richard, the fourteenth Earl of Arundel, in 1395 as a hospital/almshouse. Like Arundel College which was mentioned in Chapter 5, the Maison Dieu was built round a quadrangle. It consisted principally of a chapel, refectory and living accommodation. The establishment was run by a "Master", a priest who combined administrative and spiritual rôles. The inmates, who wore a brown woollen garment, were expected to be scrupulous in their religious observances and to engage in useful work, unless prevented by infirmity. The Maison Dieu was dissolved in 1546.

Beyond the Church is Arundel Priory, the history of which is outlined in Chapter 5. The former Oratory - the first part of the building one reaches on passing the Church - is now a theatre, the remainder, as mentioned in Chapter 5, almshouses, with a facade which is almost entirely nineteenth century work.

The route continues along London Road for a short way, and then turns to the right down New Cut (just before the High Street and opposite the road sign to Dorking and London) to Maltravers Street. Across the street to the left is the somewhat forbidding early nineteenth century Town Hall.

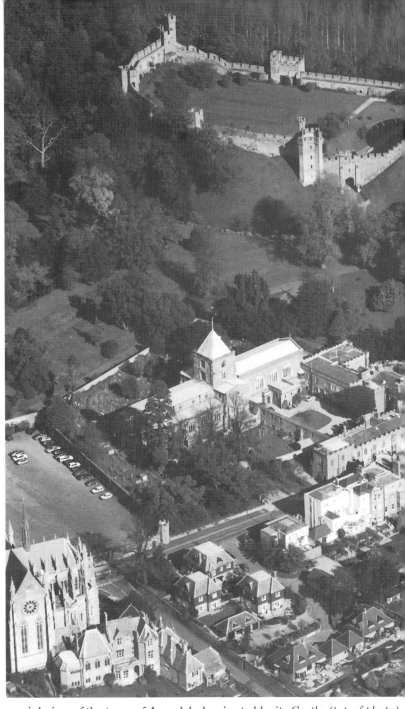

An aerial view of the town of Arundel, dominated by its Castle (top of photo)

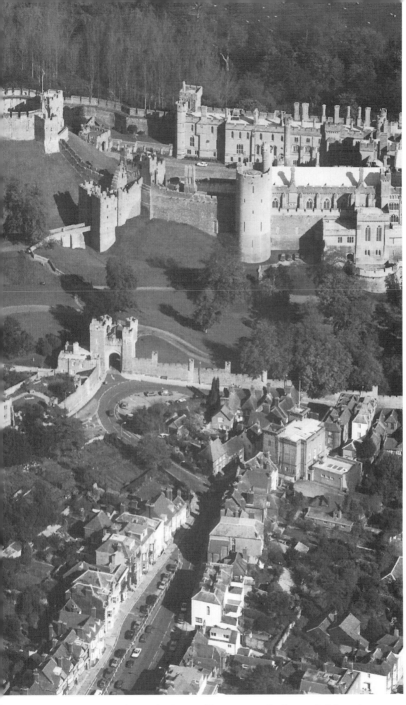

the Roman Catholic Cathedral standing out at the lower left-hand corner.

Looking over Swanbourne Lake.

Maltravers Street, which is now followed to the right, is, however, predominantly eighteenth century, the buildings showing sufficient variation to relieve what can sometimes be the monotony of the Georgian style. At No. 16 there is a plaque indicating that it was the residence of Dr. G. W. Eustace the local historian, who was author of *Arundel: Borough and Castle.*

The route continues west along Maltravers Street to its junction with Parsons Hill (running north) and Kings Arms Hill (running south). From this junction there is a good view up to the Roman Catholic Cathedral. The route follows Kings Arms Hill down to Tarrant Street.

Tarrant Street is altogether livelier than Maltravers, with shops - antique shops being a speciality - and restaurants. The route follows this Street to the left, towards the High Street.

Water adjacent to Swanbourne Lake.

Its position rising uphill from the bridge gives the High Street a certain natural excitement; in climbing it, one is rewarded with views across the Downs. The two sides of the Street differ in the character of their buildings. On the east, eighteenth century brick buildings predominate, the Norfolk Arms, a former coaching inn, providing the focus. To the west, there is much more variety of style, and roofline, with the West Sussex Gazette building a notable example of the mock-Tudor style which is such a feature of the nineteenth century phase of Arundel's development. The Arundel Museum and Heritage Centre, also on the west side, has a wide-ranging display including documents, photographs, paintings, scale models, and other exhibits illustrative of Arundel's history.

Once the High Street has been explored, the route continues over the bridge at the bottom of the hill and along the Arun to Burpham and beyond.

CHAPTER 8. Arundel to Amberley

Distance: *About six miles.*

Walking Conditions: *Mostly paths, some of which are muddy in wet weather; short distances on roads with little traffic.*

Stations: *Arundel, Amberley.*

At the far (southern) end of Arundel Bridge a path which is signposted to the left before the Bridge House Hotel is taken. The route goes through the Hotel car park then continues to the left to reach the river by a narrow path to the side of a fence surrounding the Fitzalan Swimming Pool. It follows the river past jetties with moored boats, with Arundel Castle always dominating the skyline. As the path approaches the railway, and by a National River Authority sign giving the River Arun speed limit as $5^{1/2}$ knots, it crosses a stream, controlled by a sluicegate, which winds away to flow beneath the A27 Arundel-Worthing road west of the station, and rejoins the Arun at Tortington. This stream, which marks the boundary of the parish of Arundel, represents, according to A. H. Allcroft's *Waters of Arun*, the original line followed by the Arun itself. In Allcroft's view, the course of the river which runs from where one is now standing under Arundel Bridge and past the town is completely artificial, and the following section (starting by what is now the by-pass bridge) down to Tortington represents an enlargement of the Spring Ditch, which rises at Park Bottom north-east of the town. The evidence for this theory lies in the fact that Pynham Priory (the remains of which are incorporated in a farmhouse to the east of the station) was charged with the maintenance and repair of the wooden bridge "qui est in medio pontis de Arundell". The "pontis" in question was Arundel Causeway, running from the Priory to the rising ground now marked by the southern end of the High Street. A bridge situated where Arundel Bridge now is could not be said to be "in the middle of" the causeway, but the stream claimed as the old course of the river does cross the causeway (the modern road is still so-called) at almost

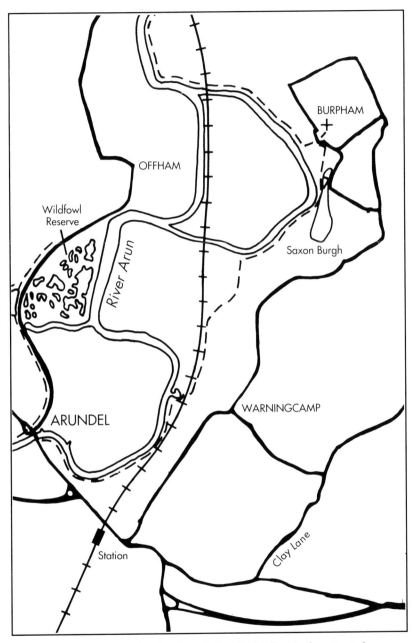

BURPHAM

OFFHAM

Wildfowl
Reserve

River Arun

Saxon Burgh

ARUNDEL

WARNINGCAMP

Station

Clay Lane

Route map, section 3: Arundel to Amberley station, part A.
Scale 1:25,000 - 2.5 inches to one mile.

exactly the right spot. The motive for the diversion of the river - thought to have been undertaken by Henry Fitzalan in the middle of the sixteenth century - would have been to make Arundel into a port.

It would be a pity for such speculation to distract one unduly from the fine scenery. Ahead is the line of the Downs; on the right is the wooded high ground of Warningcamp. With a bit of luck, there will be some swans on the river; all-in-all an idyllic scene.

Walkers can follow the river round its next loop, but the recommended route goes across the railway. Caution should be taken when crossing the line, as indicated on the notice. Just past Crossing Cottage a path indicated by a footpath sign leads off to the left of the road. The path is protected by trees and shrubs, a welcome source of shade on a hot day. Opposite a small stream a path runs to the right through a metal gate but this should not be followed. The route continues, nearly parallel with the railway on the left, until it bears right through a gate, and then turns to the left, as indicated by a signpost. The route continues with a barbed wire fence to the right and a curved line of trees to the left. It then crosses a stile on the left and continues through a field, with the direction marked by a footpath sign. It goes across a stream and then after some sixty yards turns to the left, over a stile. This route is signposted. To the right of the next section of path is a combined ditch and hedge, a tumble of hawthorns and rushes, coloured in season by loosestrife, vetch and thistle.

The next stile brings one back to the river. Here it has an aspect very different from that at Arundel, for this is not the main channel, which was diverted to the west of the railway on the construction of the line to avoid the cost of two swing bridges, but the original channel, heavily overgrown by reeds and other water-loving plants. The route continues to the right along the river. Quite suddenly one encounters steeply rising ground ahead. Having climbed a stile, it is possible to clamber up along a path, which has steps cut in it, or to continue to the left along a path which provides the recommended route. The path swerves away from the river and starts to climb. It reaches a junction in front of a fence; the turn to the right is followed into the village of Burpham.

Burpham is an idyllic English village. The scene with the Church, George

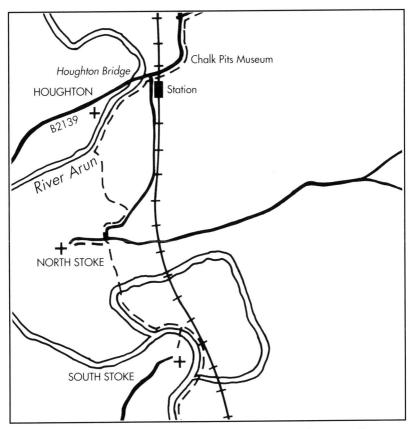

Route map, section 4: Arundel to Amberley station, part B.
Scale 1:25,000 - 2.5 inches to one mile.

and Dragon pub, thatched house, copper beech and house martins wheeling overhead is almost too good to be true. The early Norman (perhaps Saxon) Church was substantially rebuilt in the twelfth and thirteenth centuries, with additions in the nineteenth century in a happily compatible style.

What makes Burpham exceptional, however, is the fact that it is the location of the fortified site of which the steep ground to the right as one approached the village was part of the perimeter. This site took advantage of a natural chalk ridge to provide a formidable defensive position. Possibly the site was originally an Iron Age promontory fort, although there is no evidence to prove this. What is known is that Burpham was one

St. Mary's Church, Burpham.

of the "burghs" which were vital strong points in the defensive system established by Alfred the Great and his son Edward to provide protection from the Danes. The responsibility for the repair of these "burghs" and for their defence in time of war rested with the local population - a sort of early version of the Home Guard. The gateway into the site was at the same place as the current path which leads south past the George and Dragon. On both sides of the path are the remains - still formidable - of the artificial bank which protected the vulnerable north side of the fort, where it lacked the protection of naturally rising ground.

The level ground within the fort is now a recreation ground, from which there are attractive views. From the fort, the route returns past the George and Dragon and tuns to the left following downhill a small road marked by a "No Through Road" traffic sign (along which the route came into the village). The walk continues along the path, past the forge and then, where the path divides, continues to the right towards the river. Cows may be encountered along this section of the route, which follows the river bank until a ruined cottage is reached. In 1921, then still in good condition, it featured in a popular silent film called "Tansy". At this point the route crosses the stile and then turns left across another stile. The route continues alongside the river and then crosses the railway line. Particular care is needed here. Shortly past the railway line one reaches the point where the old course of the river joins the new cut. From this point the atmosphere becomes more remote and indeed lonely. Along these stretches of the river it is not difficult to imagine more turbulent times when the surrounding downs, now so domesticated, could have contained hidden menace. Such oppressive thoughts are, however, dispelled when the little hamlet of South Stoke appears on the opposite bank. Shortly before the hamlet is reached, there is marshy ground to the right of the path, and this is the point at which yet another diversion of the river took place, for this marshy tract marks the old course of the Arun and the current course represents a cut made in 1839 to bring the river closer to South Stoke and improve navigation.

A footbridge takes one over the river into South Stoke. The route follows a track bearing a little to the right which brings one to a road; a path leads to the left to St. Leonard's Church. The Church is essentially the original eleventh century building, with thirteenth century lancet windows. The nineteenth century brought "restoration" and a curious, to my mind somewhat Alpine, spire. The Church must be one of the very few left in the country without electricity; it is still lit by candles. Once when I was there sheep were grazing in the churchyard, an economical way of keeping the grass under control. The hamlet of South Stoke consists mainly of cottages, but has two buildings of substantial size whose Georgian frontages conceal an earlier origin; the Old Rectory (behind the

Looking across the river to South Stoke: the church is on the right.

east end of the Church) is fifteenth century, and South Stoke Farmhouse, overlooking the river, is sixteenth.

The route involves retracing one's steps over the bridge and turning left along a signposted path which initially follows the embankment. Shortly the footpath bears right, by a river speed limit sign, and runs through a wood, keeping on its left the old course of the river; this is the upstream end of the disused loop of which the downstream end was crossed before South Stoke was reached. The path crosses this residual stream by means of a suspension bridge. There is no footpath sign at this point, but the route goes straight up a slight hill towards buildings on the brow, which are part of North Stoke. It crosses a farm track, goes over a stile and on reaching a lane the route turns left, passes a telephone box, and follows through to the Church.

Houghton Bridge with, in the background, the chalk face above the Chalk Pits Museum.

Like its southern cousin, North Stoke is a hamlet which has the river on three sides, and is cut off from through traffic. While the churches of this part of Sussex are often notable for their evocation of the past, that at North Stoke (like St. Mary's Tortington, in the care of the Redundant Churches Fund) is exceptional in the extent to which it retains a medieval atmosphere. Built between the Norman period and the fourteenth century, it has some fine stone carving of foliage and an animal's head, floral patterns can still be seen on the walls, and the east window and south transept east window contain panels of what is said to be the oldest stained glass in Sussex. Next to the Church is Manor Farm, in Georgian style. From this point the route returns to the telephone box and then turns left along Stoke Road.

The route follows Stoke Road downhill to Sloe Cottage. Just past this point a path is signposted to the left. It is possible to continue along the road, but the recommended route runs along this path which follows what was the bank of the river before the "Houghton cut" was made at some point before 1724 - the course of the rest of that original loop of the river can be detected to the west of Stoke Road. The path is somewhat overgrown at first but when it reaches the river it provides pleasant views of Houghton on the opposite bank. The route continues to the right and runs up to Houghton Bridge, medieval in style but built in 1875. Amberley Station is to the right of the bridge.

CHAPTER 9. Amberley - Chalk Pits Museum, Castle and Village

Distance:	*About two miles.*
Walking Conditions:	*Mostly roads; a short stretch of path which is muddy in wet weather.*
	It should however be noted that this walk leads on to those in Chapters 10 and 11, with no station until Pulborough. Before attempting these walks as a sequence, account should be taken of the overall distance, and of the comments about walking conditions in Chapter 10.
Station:	*Amberley.*

From Houghton Bridge may be seen the chalk face of the hillside to the right, excavated by generations of workmen so that the chalk might be converted, by burning, into lime.

The main use of lime is as a constituent of mortar and cement, although it also serves as a fertiliser. The technique of burning chalk in kilns to make lime was known to the Romans, and there is reference in the will of the Bishop of Chichester dated 1382 to the right to dig and burn chalk at Amberley.

There is no continuous record of the chalk pits between the medieval period and the end of the eighteenth century. Early in the nineteenth century there were several separate producers working the pits. The commercial development of the site was assisted by improved access

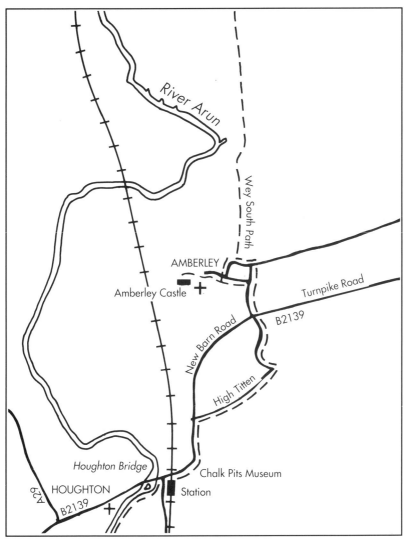

Route map, section 5: Amberley station to Amberley Wild Brooks.
Scale 1:25,000 - 2.5 inches to one mile.

through work to increase the navigability of the lower Arun and the building of the Wey and Arun Canal, and in 1863 by the coming of the railway - in 1870 a spur line gave direct access to the pits. In 1876 John Pepper, who was originally a shipowner but later a farmer and brickmaker, had along with his son Thomas taken over the business of one of

79

North Way, Amberley - Old Place in the foreground.

the established firms at the Amberley pits, and by the end of the century their firm was in possession of the whole site.

The works closed in the 1960s and have been converted into the Chalk Pits Museum, which is to the right under the railway bridge opposite the station. It would not be appropriate in this book to attempt to provide the detailed information about the Museum which is contained in the guidebook available there. It should perhaps be explained however that the Museum contains a number of exhibits, interesting in themselves, which are quite unrelated to the original site, such as the Tanyard Building, a cast-iron structure dating from 1842 which came originally from Bermondsey in south-east London. Other exhibits cover subjects

Further view of North Way, Amberley.

such as the history of radio and television, and stationary engines once used on farms and in workshops, and there is a working pottery from which a variety of articles can be bought.

On leaving the Museum, the route turns right on to the main B2139 road. Initially there is a path running parallel to the road to the left; after it ends care is needed walking along the road. Shortly before the crest of the hill, the route turns right up a minor road, High Titton. There are good views of the Downs, and of Amberley below. A path running to the right, with vehicle access barred by two wooden posts, leads to an open space which gives a "bird's eye view" of the Chalk Pits Museum. High Titton meets a lane, which is followed down the hill. Towards the bottom of the hill branches meet overhead, creating an enclosed, private world unlikely to be disturbed by the rush of traffic. At the end of the lane the road crosses over the B2139 into Amberley.

Amberley is one of the oldest settlement sites in the valley, and is first mentioned in 683. It was a centre for agricultural activity, with many of the buildings in the village having originally been used for farm purposes, and some still in such use. Its exceptional attractions have attracted artists, and it is now understandably a magnet for tourists. Perhaps there is an element of self-consciousness in its picturesqueness, but the village has certainly not commercialised itself to exploit the tourist.

One approaches Amberley passing the village's Church of England school on one's right. To the left of the lane there is a small stream, leading appropriately enough to Stream Cottage, said to have been built in 1587. Then one reaches the modest intersection known as the Square with, on the right, another sixteenth century building, Old Stack Cottage. Here the route turns left, along Church Street, a road bordered by houses of exceptional aesthetic and historical interest. On the north side is Old Postings, once the Post Office but originally built - although never used - as a butcher's shop. On the south of Church Street the buildings start with Forge Cottage, occupied by the village blacksmith till 1955; then there is the Old Brew House, which provided a service to the Vine House next door when that building was a beer house, known as the Golden Cross in the nineteenth century. Next is the Malt House, originally used, not surprisingly, as a store house for malt.

On the north side of the road, the cottages include The Old Bakehouse, the name indicating its former rôle in the life of the village, and The Studio which belonged to Gerald Burn, a painter and etcher. Back on the south side there is Drewitt's Farm, a partly flint farmhouse, followed by a public footpath to the Recreation Ground opposite North Way. After that comes Boxwood, once the home of Fred Stratton, another member of the village's artistic colony, and then The Haven, which was once a butcher's shop. The Chapel a little further on opened in 1867; it is now Amberley Village Pottery. Next door is the curious Manse, which has an oriental flavour. The route continues along the south side of Church Street, past a reed-thatched barn. Next to the barn is Oak Tree House. The House is formed from three former cottages; the one at the east end used to house the Clarkson Room, where one of the first Dame's Schools in Amberley was established in the middle of the nineteenth century.

Beyond Oak Tree House is the Vicarage, situated behind the Church Hall. The Vicarage was completely rebuilt in the first half of the eighteenth century, although Elizabethan cellars remain. The Church Hall was built in 1964, replacing two successive earlier buildings on the site.

It is thought that there was a Saxon Church at Amberley, but no trace of it remains. St. Michael's Church was originally built under the direction of Bishop Luffa, the founder of Chichester Cathedral, in about 1100. The nave and roof survive from that building. It was expanded in the latter half of the twelfth century, the large north and west windows dating from that time. The long chancel, with its lancet windows typical of Sussex churches, is thirteenth century, from which the tower is also thought to date. Although the Church is not without impressive qualities, it does not to my mind have the same atmosphere as some of the others in the area.

Past the Church, a path runs under the formidable curtain wall of Amberley Castle and the route follows this. The wall, with the gatehouse, was built about 1380, when defensive measures were considered necessary against the French and also, it seems possible, against the local peasantry! It protected an earlier manor house, probably twelfth century, which is now at the south-east corner of the complex. The west side of this building - facing into the courtyard - is most attractive.

The Castle has had a varied history. It was founded, like the Church, by Bishop Luffa, and it was Bishop Rede who fortified it, and also built the Great Hall. This building - much of which has been demolished - lies on a north-south alignment behind the kitchen which is the easterly, and most substantial, projection from the north wall, and was originally attached to the manor house. It appears that the last Bishop of Chichester to live at the Castle was Robert Sherburne (1508 - 1536); in 1538 the Castle was let to Sir William Shelley and Sir William Goring. During the Civil War John Goring held it for the Royalists, and it has been claimed that the Castle was sacked by Parliamentary forces, although there appears to be no evidence for this.

A view of Amberley Castle from the air. Still very largely intact, the old warl
now surrounded by peaceful agricultural land and (to t

le walls are closely adjoined by the Church on the right. These buildings are
ht in the photo) the pleasant houses of Amberley village.

Amberley Castle gatehouse.

The lease changed hands frequently after that time, by sale as well as by succession, until the Castle was sold outright in 1872 to Lord Zouche of Parham, and then purchased by the Duke of Norfolk in 1893. In 1925 Thomas Emmet became the owner, being succeeded by his widow, who was created a life Peeress. The Castle is now a hotel.

From the end of the Castle wall one returns along the path and then continues along the north (left) side of Church Street, past Amberley House, built in 1911 by an American. The lane leading to the left, known as The Alley (formerly Smock Alley) is worth exploring. Naillards, on the

A view of the interior of Amberley Castle showing, on the right, the manor house.

right of The Alley as one walks up, is called after a family of that name. After The Alley, the route continues along the north side of Church Street to North Way (formerly known more picturesquely as Hog Lane), which is then followed. On the left as one turns up North Way is Old Place, formed from the combination of three or four cottages. Stott's Cottage, opposite, is named after the artist Edward Stott who lived there.

As North Way turns to the right, a path leads off to the left; this is the next direction the recommended route will take. Before following that path, however, it is worth exploring Amberley a little further. On the right of North Way is the thatched North Road Farmhouse. Beyond that, running downhill from the Black Horse, is the delightfully-named High Street, with little in common with the many suburban roads known by that name. On the left hand side is the village shop.

Retracing one's steps, one comes back to the already-mentioned path from North Way leading into Amberley Wild Brooks, one of those wetlands which are a diminishing feature of our landscape.

CHAPTER 10. Amberley to Hardham Church

Distance:	About three and a half miles.
Walking Conditions:	Paths, mostly quite firm, but one section marshy as explained below; a stretch of busy road.
Stations:	None.

The route runs straight on into the Brooks. The area is one of rough grassland and drainage ditches, sometimes flooded in winter, and supports a considerable variety of wildlife. Drainage of the area has been proposed, but a public enquiry in 1978 rejected the idea: a notable success for the conservationists. It should be said that the path through the northern part of the Brooks is muddy even in dry weather, and can be very difficult during periods of heavy rains. Stout footwear is always desirable on this route, and in the winter walking through the marshy area may well be impracticable, and it would be advisable then to pick up at a later stage the route suggested in this chapter.

The path on the original route is initially firm and chalky, but in due course it comes to consist of an earth embankment raised above the level of the surrounding fields. The route continues past a sign marked "Caution-Dangerous Marsh". Some distance ahead, the main path turns left. The route continues ahead over a stile. Two small wooden bridges take the route across drainage channels and then a field is reached and is crossed, keeping a fence on the left. At the top (left) corner the route goes through a metal barred gate (please leave gates open or shut as you find them). The route turns to the right through another gate just by a new wooden house on stone foundations. Where the path meets another at a T-junction, the route turns left. The route runs through a farmyard and continues to follow the path until it divides. The left fork is taken over a cattle grid. As the Arun comes into sight on the left a grassy path leads off along it, to Greatham Bridge.

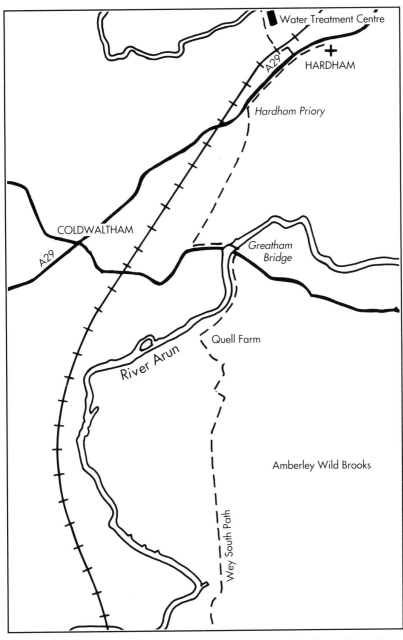

Route map, section 6: Amberley Wild Brooks to Hardham Church.
Scale 1:25,000 - 2.5 inches to one mile.

This bridge was built between 1307 and 1327 by Sir Henry Tregoz, the Lord of the Manor of Greatham. The western half has been little altered since that date; the eastern half has been cut away, and the piers now carry iron girders, with an unfortunate effect on the overall appearance of the bridge.

The course of the river under Greatham Bridge marks yet another of the human interventions in the Arun's course. Originally the river flowed (on a line indicated by the current parish boundary between Parham and Coldwaltham) along a meander which ended just below Greatham Bridge, remaining south of the Greatham - Coldwaltham road until it crossed it at the point where the road now intersects with the disused canal described later. The river then followed a course north-west almost to the village of Coldwaltham, where it turned to the north-east at the far side of where the railway line now runs. It then looped below the higher ground on which Hardham Priory stands to turn south, joining the current course of the river less than half a mile north of Greatham Bridge. This lost meander of the Arun was known as the Widney, and the meadows between it and the current main stream of the river remained known as "The Widneys". There is no certain information about when the present route of the river under Greatham Bridge was cut, but it seems reasonable to suppose that it was at the same time as the bridge was built.

From Greatham Bridge, a short walk along the road brings one to a concrete and tubular steel fence on the right which marks where the road crosses the route of the disused canal. This canal was built in 1785 and ran from a point almost a mile south of Greatham Bridge up to Hardham Mill on the River Rother close to its junction with the Arun, to save three miles on the Arun route through Pulborough. In spite of the advantage given by the shortening of the route, it is quite surprising that anyone should have embarked on the construction of this stretch of canal given the substantial obstacle of a ridge which had to be overcome. A quarter-mile long tunnel was dug under the ridge. J. B. Dashwood, in his *The Thames to the Solent* (1868), an amusing account of a boating trip from the Thames at Weybridge to the South Coast via the Wey and Arun Canal, describes going through this tunnel. He punted the boat along by means of a boat-hook against the roof, which was covered with stalactites, and it took about ten minutes to reach the far end.

Greatham Bridge.

There is a stile towards the end of the fence (to the right of the road) mentioned in the previous paragraph and this is crossed to follow the path along the left side of the old canal. This path is rather overgrown, although not difficult to walk. A wooden bridge over a ditch is crossed. Further on, the route follows a stile into a field, from which Hardham Priory is visible on the right. This Priory was founded by Sir William Dawtrey in the reign of Henry II. It was a small establishment, seeming never to have had more than six inmates. The Priors seem to have been unduly subject to the distractions of the world, including the opposite sex. One was deposed and another sent to Tortington Priory to reflect on the errors of his ways. In 1524, the then Prior admitted that he had stolen deer from the Earl of Arundel. The Priory was dissolved and sold in 1534.

The Priory buildings are now part of a farm complex and are private property without access to the public. Nevertheless, the route along the old canal does provide good views, particularly of the Chapter House, with its fine lancet windows.

The remains of Hardham Priory.

The route continues along the side of the old canal until the southern entrance of the tunnel mentioned earlier can be seen. The route runs up a slope into a field which is crossed to a gate leading to the A19, and it turns right along the road in the direction of Pulborough. A walk of about half a mile brings one to the hamlet of Hardham, which is set along a winding street a little back from the main road. The Church is probably Saxon, for it is dedicated to St. Botolph, the Saxon patron of ports and river crossings (appropriate as the Church is so near Pulborough Bridge), and has the traditional Saxon square East End. The small windows high in the nave and chancel are also Saxon in character - the other windows are later, and the bell-turret and porch are Victorian. Roman tiles and bricks were used in the building of the Church - these probably came from the nearby Roman site.

The outstanding feature of the Church is the series of wall paintings dating from around 1100. Unhappily the paintings were seriously damaged in 1860s, first when the plaster was chipped away to expose them, then through preservation work which lacked the techniques available today. Nevertheless, enough remains for it to be possible to envisage the effect when the paintings were complete and in their original bright colours. The leaflet *Hardham - its History and its Church,* available in the Church, lists the paintings, which illustrate biblical stories and other scenes thought to offer spiritual edification.

One picture shows Eve milking a cow, although the animal bears more resemblance to a large greyhound. Another is of St. George and probably represents the legend of his intervention at the Battle of Antioch in 1098. The Crusaders' victory at Antioch was a decisive event which cleared the way to the advance on Jerusalem. One of the leaders of the First Crusade was Robert of Normandy, the eldest son of William the Conqueror. By one of the small ironies of history, the Crusaders at Antioch were considerably assisted by siege materials brought by Edgar the Atheling, the exiled Saxon claimant to the English throne.

What did the Saxon people who first saw these paintings, for some of whom the Battle of Hastings must have been a living memory, know or make of such events? We can only guess; but the unity of Christendom at that time was no doubt regarded as transcending such political differences.

For us today, the different artistic influences which may be traced in the Hardham wall paintings, Anglo-Saxon, French, and Byzantine, are a reminder of the cosmopolitan nature of early medieval culture. Unsophisticated the Hardham painter may have been, but not parochial; he was working in a European tradition. He could also draw on a body of belief shared with the people who saw his work - an advantage which some painters of our own time might envy.

St. Botolph's Church, Hardham.

CHAPTER 11. Hardham Church to Pulborough

Distance: *About four and a quarter miles.*

Walking Conditions: *Paths, mostly firm; stretches of road, some busy.*

Station: *Pulborough.*

From Hardham it is possible to continue along the busy A29 into Pulborough, but the recommended route involves returning along the A29 to a road off to the right with a level crossing with automatic barriers sign. This road crosses the railway line and runs through the middle of the Southern Water Services Treatment Works. The Works takes water from the River Rother shortly before it joins the Arun; supplies can also be drawn from boreholes. Supplanting the Rother Pumping Station, the Works was opened in July 1985 by the late Ian Gow, M.P., the then Minister for Housing and Construction. It is highly computerised, and serves much of West Sussex north of the South Downs, including Horsham and Crawley. A little beyond the railway line, the road crosses the line of Stane Street, the Roman road from Chichester to London, although it is not visible at this point.

The route continues straight along towards a bridge over the River Rother; on the left hand side of the road, just before the bridge, are the remains of Hardham Mill. After the bridge the route goes straight on over a stile by footpath and Pulborough District Angling Society signs. It then crosses a field to a rustic-looking bridge over the Arun to the left of a concrete structure which also arches over the river. At the near end of the bridge, looking back, to the right of the Treatment Works, may be seen the location of a Roman "mansio".

This mansio is thought to have been established within ten years of the conquest by Aulus Plautius (which, as mentioned in the Introduction, took place in 43 AD). The mansiones were fortified posts, important links

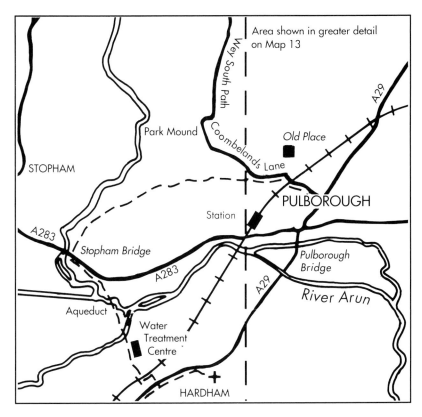

Route map, section 7: Hardham Church to Pulborough.
Scale 1:25,000 - 2.5 inches to one mile.

in the system of Roman communications. Excavations at the Hardham mansio indicated that there was a barracks for the troops who patrolled the road, as well as accommodation and stabling for those using Stane Street for state or commercial purposes. The mansio had a vallum - an earth wall - with a stockade, later improved by the addition of masonry walls at corners, and measured 420 feet by 435 feet. Pottery remains suggest the continuation of a pre-existing pottery works; remains of burials confirmed that this site was occupied by Belgic people before the Romans arrived. After being used for about a century, the mansio was abandoned. Unhappily, when the now-derelict branch line to Midhurst was built it cut through the centre of the remains of the building. It has been suggested that the abandonment of the Hardham mansio was followed by the establishment of a new one on a site east of Pulborough Church in the approximate position of the modern Rectory; but this has not been proved.

The route takes one over the bridge and then to the left along the Arun, an idyllic scene at this spot. To the left is the entrance to the canal cut, built in 1794, which linked the Rivers Rother and Arun as part of the Rother Navigation to Petworth and Midhurst. The route then turns right to a stile next to a rusty barred gate. This leads to what was once the A283, but is now a minor road following construction of the new Stopham Bridge. This road is followed to the White Hart.

This attractive public house stands at the east end of Stopham Bridge, good views of which may be obtained from the garden. Originally there was a ford at this site; it was replaced by a ferry, known as the Estover Ferry. The first bridge dated from the mid fourteenth century, and was probably of wood. In 1423 it was rebuilt in stone, and it remains unchanged to this day, with the exception of the centre arch, which was raised in 1822 to provide additional headroom for sailing craft. Stopham Bridge is a fine piece of architecture, much enhanced by its delightful setting. On the west bank of the river, party hidden by trees, is Stopham House. There have been houses at this site at least since Tudor times, but the present house is as remodelled in 1865 by Sir Walter Barttelot, whose ancestor John Barttelot acquired the Manor by marriage in the fifteenth century.

Stopham Bridge is now for use by pedestrians only, as a by-pass and new bridge north of the old one were completed in June 1986. Some may feel that the proximity of the new bridge detracts from the beauty of the setting of the old one; on the other hand, the protection of Stopham Bridge from the rigours of modern traffic was obviously a very desirable step from the point of view of the preservation of its structure.

From Stopham Bridge, the route crosses the A283 near the new bridge, to a path marked by a sign "Dogs must be kept on a lead in these woodlands". The path climbs out of the valley; the walker can enjoy the smell of pine. After a short while, it skirts the edge of the woodland area; to the right, across the fields, are views of the Downs; the tower of

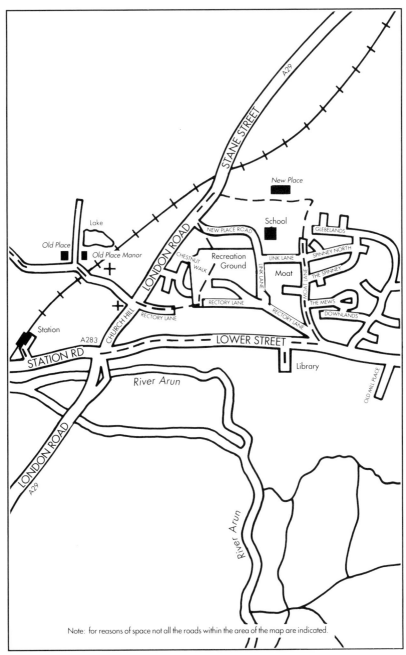

Town map of Pulborough. Scale 1:15,840 - 4 inches to one mile.

The buildings of Old Place, Pulborough, and the adjoini

100

d Place Manor seen from the air looking eastwards.

Pulborough Church can be seen through trees. Faint traffic noise from the road below only slightly disturbs the peaceful scene. The route passes a fine stretch of pines to the left. A path leading off to the right is not taken, nor is a later one to the left; the line of the fence is followed. The route goes by the side of a five-barred wooden gate, down a grey gravel path, and then goes straight across a lane. In the next field is a well-preserved Second World War concrete defensive position, once occupied no doubt in much the same spirit as that in which the Anglo-Saxons looked to the defence of Burpham.

The route follows downhill until it reaches Coombelands Lane. It then turns right along the Lane. On the left are Old Place and Old Place Manor, attractive fifteenth century buildings. Old Place, the first to be reached, was originally a barn. With its mullioned windows, well-kept garden, and lake behind, it has an idyllic air. Once when I was there I saw a heron which was perched on a pontoon in the middle of the lake, so still that for a moment I wondered whether it was a sculpture, until it took off in majestic flight. Old Place Manor is best viewed from the far end of the lake. While interesting, it lacks the idiosyncratic, evocative quality of Old Place.

Old Place Manor dates from the reign of Henry VI (1422-61) and was built by Nicholas Apsley, although it has been subjected to substantial alteration. Old Place (also altered) may well date from the same time. The name of Apsley is now remembered because of Apsley House in London, which was built (1771-78) by the architect Robert Adam for Baron Apsley (subsequently Earl Bathurst), who was descended from Nicholas Apsley. Apsley House was bought by the Duke of Wellington's elder brother, and subsequently by the Duke himself, as whose home it became famous as No 1 London. Apsley House now faces the swirling traffic of Hyde Park Corner; there could be no greater contrast to the peaceful surroundings of Old Place.

The road is followed over the railway. A little further on is St Mary's Church, which one approaches through the fourteenth century lychgate. The Church was originally Norman, but only the font survives from that time. The chancel is thought to be late twelfth or thirteenth century, while the nave, aisles and tower date from 1420-30, and are in characteristic

Perpendicular style. There is an oak screen by Sir Ninian Comper at the west end of the nave.

Past the Church, the route crosses the busy London Road into Rectory Lane, past the Chequers Hotel on the left. The lane passes the fine Old Rectory, built by the Rev. Francis Mose, Rector from 1720-1729. Past the Old Rectory is a dovecote originally in the Rectory garden. A little further on is the Glebe Barn. The route continues along the footpath and turns left past the bowling green to the Recreation Ground, crossing it towards a housing estate, the rugby pitch being kept on the right and the cricket square on the left. As one approaches the houses, one discovers to the left what is described on a notice as a "Pocket Park" running along a stream. This park represents a most commendable initiative, providing a pleasant stroll, with a fine display of daffodils in spring. The path through the park leads on to New Place Road and then to London Road.

A few paces to the right along the London Road bring one to a minor road running to the right past signs saying "New Place Nurseries Quality Plants" and "Public Bridleway". This path is followed past allotments on the right.

A high wall on the left protects the former Manor House of New Place. In about 1450 this building, as part of the manor, came into the hands of Nicholas Apsley, already mentioned in connection with Old Place Manor. New Place as it now stands (and it is not open to the public) is predominantly sixteenth century. There is a gateway through which Elizabeth I is said to have passed when visiting the Apsley family in 1591 - that gateway is thought to have formed the entrance to a quadrangle, three sides of which were occupied by the mansion. Among the features of New Place is a curious chimney with a mullioned window at its base. In 1732, John Apsley sold the building to Henry Shelley of Lewes, who was related to the Horsham Shelleys who produced the poet. On the death of John Apsley, Old Place Manor passed to Francis Mose of Petworth, thereby ending the Apsley connection with Pulborough.

The route runs along a path to the right of, and then between, plastic greenhouses. Past the greenhouses the path meets another at right angles to it; the route turns right at the junction, and follows the tree-lined

Old Place - view from the north-west.

path past a new housing development (Glebelands) on the left and St. Mary's Church of England School on the right. The path continues across a road into Moat Lane. There is an open space to the right and some forty yards across it a moat duly appears. Within the area of the moat are grass and trees, with no indication of any building which may have stood there. It is possible that this is the site of the precursor of New Place; in 1251 Alard de Fleming was granted a licence to rebuild his house at Pulborough, perhaps within the bounds of this moat.

The route returns to Moat Lane. As one follows it over a rise, there are fine views over the Downs. Moat Lane runs into Rectory Lane, which itself leads on the left into Lower Street. The route turns right at this point. Past the Oddfellows Arms the route follows a short road leading to the Public Library - few libraries can have such a fine view, for there is a panorama of the Arun plain and the Downs. The route continues back to Lower Street and along it to the left. Across the mini-roundabout where Church Hill (A29) runs off to the right there are two attractive 400-year-old timber framed cottages, Skye Cottage and Horncroft. The route continues to the left round by Corden's, a chemist's shop with a pleasant old-fashioned atmosphere; the shop was previously a public house called The Running Horse.

The A29 (here the London Road) runs over a modern bridge, built in 1936. The earlier bridge, built in 1738 to replace a wooden one, remains alongside and is open to pedestrians. There was originally another eighteenth century bridge in Pulborough, Clement Bridge, which was close to the railway bridge, but this was demolished in the 1930s.

The route does not go over the bridge but continues past The Parrot along Station Road (A283) to Pulborough Station, where this series of walks ends. It has encompassed a wide variety of scene, built-up and rural, and has provided much opportunity for reflection on the complex natural and historical forces which lie behind what presents itself to our eyes. The past was not one long idyll, rudely interrupted by the modern world; it contained much violence, poverty and disease, as well as those happier features, such as a strong sense of community, which we now so often miss. I hope that this book has helped, to however small a degree, appreciation of the area it describes, and perhaps even of wider aspects of our inheritance.

BIBLIOGRAPHICAL NOTE

It would be quite impracticable to list here all the books and other sources which have a bearing on the subject matter of this book. I should however like to make special acknowledgement of three books which I have found of particular value in writing *Along the Arun.*

Waters of Arun by A. H. Allcroft, Methuen, 1930.

This book is a classic of its type, full of erudition and sharp observation, as well as illuminating and sometimes quirky speculation. It is essentially a history of the Arun, particularly strong on the changes of course of the river. Writers who research the Arun must find themselves in debt to Mr Allcroft, and can only hope that they have not fallen too far below his standard of scholarship and freshness of approach.

The Arun and Western Rother by Robert H. Goodsall, Constable, 1962.

This is essentially a guide book, and one which covers a considerably wider geographical area than my own book, as it traces the Arun from its sources, and also the Western Rother from its source near Selborne to its junction with the Arun at Hardham.

BIBLIOGRAPHICAL NOTE *(continued)*

The Dukes of Norfolk, A Quincentennial History by John Martin Robinson, Oxford University Press, 1982.

This work is a model of what a family history should be and stands as a definitive treatment of its subject. I have relied heavily on it in writing about the Howards in Chapter 4.

For readers who wish to follow up subjects mentioned in this book, *Local History of West Sussex - A Guide to Sources* by Kim C. Leslie and Timothy J. McCann (1971, 2nd revised edition 1975) provides an admirable guide to sources. In addition, since the early 1970s Sussex Bibliographies have appeared at intervals, many published by the Sussex Archaeological Society, and these may be consulted at the West Sussex Record Office, County Hall, Chichester, or at the Library of the Sussex Archaeological Society at Barbican House, Lewes.